HUMAN KNOWING

JAMES W. FELT, S.J.

HUMAN KNOWING

A Prelude to Metaphysics

UNIVERSITY OF NOTRE DAME PRESS   NOTRE DAME, INDIANA

Excerpt from "Little Gidding" in *Four Quartets,* copyright © 1942 by
T. S. Eliot and renewed 1970 by Esme Valerie Eliot, reprinted by
permission of Harcourt, Inc.

Gerard Manley Hopkins, S.J., "Poem 91," from *The Poems of Gerard
Manley Hopkins,* edited by W. H. Garner and N. H. Mackenzie (London,
1989), 129–30, used by permission of Oxford University Press.

Manufactured in the United States of America

Library of Congress Cataloging-in-Publication Data
Felt, James W., 1926–
Human knowing : a prelude to metaphysics / James W. Felt.
p. cm.
Includes bibliographical references and index.
ISBN 0-268-02878-8 (hardcover : alk. paper)
ISBN 0-268-02879-6 (pbk. : alk. paper)
1. Knowledge, Theory of. I. Title.
BD161.F387   2005
121—dc22
2005019661

∞ This book is printed on acid-free paper.

For W. Norris Clarke, S.J.

CONTENTS

PREFACE

In an *"Epistle to the Reader"* John Locke begins his *Essay Concerning Human Understanding* by acknowledging that it may appear prideful that he publishes something he thinks others might profit from reading. He retorts however that it would be arrogant to publish for any other reason. The following short essay, elementary though it is, was written for that same reason. It has grown out of almost five decades of philosophic engagement with teachers, colleagues, and students on a topic critical to understanding oneself and the world. Those who can't make philosophic sense of their immediate experience of encountering trees and puppies and people wind up supposing themselves confined within an illusory world of appearances. That is the very misconception that for three and a half centuries has mainly dominated Western philosophy, and I propose to put something better in its place. The key to making philosophic sense out of how you constantly rub shoulders with a world of real objects lies in rethinking what is going on in your sensing and knowing, without buying into the misconceived ways in which this problem has usually been thought of since the seventeenth century.

The account that I shall argue for is not so much new as the result of rethinking, in the light of more modern insights, the analysis of Thomas Aquinas. My own philosophic perspective is heavily influenced by Aquinas, Bergson, Whitehead, and perhaps Merleau-Ponty, but all these strands of thought have grown so intertwined and taken for granted in my own thinking that I despair, after so many years, of distinctly recognizing let alone properly acknowledging my own intellectual debts. I do wish however to express special gratitude to my former teachers, especially Richard J. Blackwell of Saint Louis University, to my wise and good friend, Fr. W. Norris Clarke of Fordham University, and to the readers of the earlier draft of this essay for most helpful suggestions.

chapter 1

INVITATION TO A PHILOSOPHIC EXPLORATION

Come on an introductory philosophic inquiry into one of the most remarkable and mysterious abilities we have: our power of knowing. By it we relate ourselves to the world and the world to us in a whole spectrum of activities ranging from sense perception through science to philosophic knowing.[1] We shall be exploring what is happening in these activities as understood from a philosophic perspective. Put in more technical terms, this excursion amounts to a brief introduction to epistemology that is also an invitation to metaphysics.

I should mention at the outset that I have deliberately entitled this an essay on *human* knowing. We shall have enough to do just to interpret our own firsthand knowing without venturing into speculation about such things as animal consciousness. The reader may wish to make those extrapolations later.

1.1 ON ASKING PHILOSOPHIC QUESTIONS

What is a philosophic perspective, and what is it to ask a philosophic question? That is just to ask what it is to engage in philosophy.

---

1. I shall not here attempt to examine aesthetic, moral, or religious knowing.

Philosophy is an activity of the human mind by which we inquire into the ultimate intelligible structure of the world of our experience, including that experience itself. It is an investigation into the ultimate nature and meaning of the experienced world and of our experience of it, an attempt to understand experience in its dimension of value and meaning. That is what Aristotle called "first philosophy," first in the sense of the most fundamental kind of knowing. Thus, contrary to a widely held contemporary view, this discussion will presume that philosophy is more than a matter of untangling the knots we may have tied in our way of talking about things. Philosophy intends, sometimes successfully, to illuminate the world, not just our language.

More specifically, our philosophic inquiry will first examine sense perception both as it seems to give itself to us and as it has largely been interpreted by philosophers of the last three hundred years (chapter 2). In the third chapter we shall probe more deeply into the intrinsic structure of perception, and in the fourth we shall discover the philosophic foundations underlying that structure. In chapter five we pass beyond perception to the general aspects of the activity of *understanding* what is given us in perception (ordinary knowing). In chapter six we shall glimpse that special kind of knowing that is scientific knowing, and in chapter seven explore the nature of philosophic knowing as exemplified in the thought of four of the greatest philosophers of the last 2400 years. Finally, in chapter eight, we shall examine whether the philosophic enterprise itself, and as exemplified in these thinkers, deserves the name of knowledge.

This may seem like too much to attempt in one slender essay, and perhaps it is. But as G. K. Chesterton somewhere remarked, if a thing is worth doing it is worth doing badly. Even a sketchy understanding of our ways of knowing is better than none at all, and better in the long run than an exhaustive analysis of just one of them. But let me make two preliminary observations.

First, the "knowing" that we shall explore is meant in a broad sense, to include all kinds of acts of human cognition, beginning with bodily sensing and ending perhaps in some form of intuition.

Second, in what follows I do not speak so much to fellow philosophers as to all intelligent readers curious about their own acts of knowing, regardless of whether they have a formal background in philosophy. Even if this is your first experience in philosophic thinking, this essay is written for you. Discussions among professional philosophers about these matters have become so technical and complex that it is almost impossible for a nonprofessional to see the forest for the trees. And though the conclusions reached here will be derived in a non-technical way, I hold that they are both philosophically sound and well grounded in the philosophic tradition. True, they will not likely change the minds of any fellow philosophers who hold principles that disagree with those I shall propose, but the conclusions are no less plausible for all that. There is no clean-cut certainty to be had about philosophic positions, otherwise there would not be so much disagreement about them. You the reader will have to decide for yourself whether the method adopted and the conclusions reached agree with what you find when you reflect on your own experience.

It is worth noting at the outset that a philosophic inquiry is distinct from a scientific one. Philosophy explicitly includes the dimension of value and meaning in experience, and that dimension lies outside the bounds of science. Philosophy aims to include the whole of human experience, not just selected aspects of it. It reflects on our experience of beauty and of moral worth and of friendship, and it does not try to account for them in the narrower terms of atoms in motion or DNA.

But just here there arises a challenge to this whole investigation that I have proposed, a challenge that must be taken seriously. It is this: Has not modern science rendered a philosophic inquiry into knowing obsolete? Don't the remarkable recent advances in understanding the biological and neurological functions of the brain, together with advancing speculations about "artificial intelligence," prove that knowing of all sorts is just brain activity? Isn't philosophic speculation about knowing simply an exercise in futility, a relic of an age of myth that has been superseded by science? This challenge calls for an explicit reply before we go further.

1.2   HUMAN KNOWING IS DISTINCT FROM BRAIN ACTIVITY.

The first thing to notice about statement 1.2 is that it is not a scientific statement. It is in fact an example of what we have just called a philosophic statement. It makes an interpretative claim about the sort of activity that is human knowing and the sort that is brain activity, and asserts that they are distinctly different activities and so fall under different types of explanation. To state that some activity is not explicable solely in the terms available to science is to stand outside science, not to make a statement within it. Science can and does, in a most remarkable fashion, examine what goes on within the human brain, but its arena of discourse is limited to the material processes of the brain. As a consequence it is impossible to prove scientifically either the truth or the falsity of statement 1.2. Within limits, science can furnish evidence that makes 1.2 seem plausible or implausible, but you accept it or reject it not as a scientist but as a philosopher. For everyone sometimes—perhaps often—makes philosophic decisions, even the scientist.

Statement 1.2 is not only not a scientific statement, it implicitly denies that the only legitimate means to knowing lies in the methods of science. It rejects *epistemological reductionism,* the doctrine that all legitimate knowing must be an instance of scientific knowing.[2] It also implicitly denies *metaphysical* reductionism, the doctrine that all reality is material. Both these views are nothing-but-isms that are easily asserted but impossible to prove.

As to the further content of statement 1.2, it is beyond dispute that human knowing depends upon, in the sense of is always correlated with, appropriate brain functioning. They go together. The obvious conclusion might seem to be that they are either

2. Examples of such reductionism abound in contemporary discussion. Paul M. Churchland, for instance, when considering "propositional attitudes"—that is, beliefs, desires, fears, etc.—writes: "It remains an empirical question whether the propositional attitudes are ultimately physical in nature" (*Matter and Consciousness,* 66). Similarly, when considering whether religious experience might serve as evidence against identifying knowing with brain activity, Churchland remarks that the appeal to religion "can only be as good as the scientific credentials of the religion(s) being appealed to" (ibid., 14).

identical, or that brain functioning *causes* consciousness. But there is another possibility. It is at least logically possible that appropriate brain activity is a *necessary condition* for human knowing but is neither identical with it nor is its cause. It is possible that human knowing is a radically different kind of activity from brain activity even though it depends upon it as a necessary condition.

To repeat: the bare fact that knowing depends upon brain activity does not of itself prove that knowing either is identical with brain activity or is its effect. How then shall we decide whether there is an identity here, or a causal relation, or only some other functional dependence of two different sorts of activities? The philosopher John Searle, of whom we shall see more, notes that when we have noticed that two things are correlated, we still have not explained their correlation, in particular as to whether or not it is causal. (Notice that by saying "two things," Searle implicitly rejects simply identifying consciousness with brain states.) He goes on to say: "One way to try to figure out whether the correlates are causally related to each other is to try to manipulate one variable and see what happens to the other."[3] Suppose then that you find that consciousness always accompanies a certain state of affairs (in our case this would be what I have above called "appropriate brain functioning") and is always absent without it. "If you have gone that far," he writes, "then it seems to me that you have something more than a correlation, you have good evidence for a causal relation."[4]

Well, you have good evidence *either* for a causal relation between consciousness and the brain state, *or* you have evidence that the brain state is a *necessary condition* for the conscious state. Here is an example of a correlation that involves a necessary condition but not causality. Think of an air traffic controller attentive to his or

3. John Searle, *The Mystery of Consciousness,* 196.
4. Ibid., 196-97. Searle makes the first correlate even stronger by speaking of "inducing" it and thereby inducing states of consciousness. But since I suppose that neither he nor I know how one could induce the appropriate brain state, I have thought it better, and I hope still fair, simply to say that whenever we do in fact have the appropriate brain state we have the corresponding state of consciousness, and whenever we don't, we don't.

her radar screen. If the radar equipment is working properly, then an airplane coming within range is the (partial) cause of a blip's appearing on the screen, and that blip is then *interpreted* by the controller to represent an airplane. As far as the controller is concerned, a blip means a plane, no blips means no planes. But though the plane partially causes the blip, it does not *cause* the interpretation of the controller, it is only a necessary condition for it. The controller's act of *interpreting the meaning* of the blip is nothing at all like seeing the blip; it is a quite distinct activity.

In the case of consciousness, if brain activity doesn't causally account for knowing, maybe it doesn't account for it at all. Perhaps knowing, in itself, is a different type of activity altogether even though it is functionally dependent upon brain activity. And this, indeed, seems to me to be what the evidence points to, as we shall gradually see in the whole course of the following discussion.

The conviction that knowing is distinct from brain activity will arise from reflection on the evident characteristics of our own experience of knowing as they reveal themselves to deliberate reflection. There may be no single fact that would compellingly prove the truth of statement 1.2. The conviction expressed in 1.2 arises rather from a convergence of experiential pointers, several of which we shall begin to explore in the rest of this chapter. As a result, we shall find that it is at least arguable that 1.2 is correct, and so we shall be provisionally justified in continuing our investigation of various kinds of knowing without simply handing them over to neurobiologists. The further stages of our investigation will, I think, taken as a whole, powerfully confirm 1.2. Before we undertake that investigation, however, it is helpful to notice the context in which much current discussion on human knowing takes place.

1.2.1   Of consciousness and brain states

The last twenty-five years have seen an outpouring of philosophical books and essays speculating on the relation between human consciousness and brain activities. I shall mention—and not attempt here to describe in any detail—just two views that stand pretty much at opposite ends of the spectrum. These two views will clarify, by contrast, the opinion that I shall be supporting in what follows.

In 1991 Daniel Dennett published a big and much discussed book with the confident title, *Consciousness Explained.* For some philosophers the book would more accurately have been entitled "Consciousness Explained Away," because Dennett basically maintains that all conscious states, all states of knowing and feeling, are analyzable, without remainder, into complex behaviors and tendencies of the brain. To know or to feel or to love just *is* to have these certain brain activities. (We have already noted that same sort of view in Paul Churchland.) The common attitude that our conscious states are somehow irreducibly different is attributed by Dennett to "folk psychology," which, as scientifically up-to-date persons, we would want to discard.

The other view I wish to mention is that of John Searle. In *The Mystery of Consciousness,* for instance, he takes issue with Dennett chiefly by insisting that conscious states such as knowing are ontologically distinct from brain states, especially in their first-person character which can't be duplicated in the third-person terms of science. He asks:

> Why can't we reduce consciousness to neuronal behavior in the same way that we can reduce solidity to molecular behavior, for example? The short answer is this: consciousness has a first-person or subjective ontology and so cannot be reduced to anything that has a third-person or objective ontology. If you try to reduce or eliminate one in favor of the other you leave something out. What I mean by saying that consciousness has a first-person ontology is this: biological brains have a remarkable biological capacity to produce experiences, and these experiences only exist when they are felt by some human or animal agent. You can't reduce these first-person subjective experiences to third-person phenomena for the same reason that you can't reduce phenomena to subjective experiences. You can neither reduce the neuron firings to the feelings nor the

feelings to the neuron firings, because in each case you would leave out the objectivity or subjectivity that is in question.[5]

So far so excellent. But Searle is also intent on avoiding any kind of *dualism,* especially mind-body dualism. An ultimate case of this is found in René Descartes' (1596–1650) *ontological* or *substance* dualism, in which he thought of the human person as made up of two distinctly different substances: a mind, and a body that is essentially extension. He thought of mind and body as two distinctly different kinds of substance, just as he thought of circle and square as distinctly different. For the essence of mind is to be a substance that thinks, whereas the essence of body is to be spread out in space. This left Descartes with the obvious problem of how to think of a human being as one substance, as he really wished to do, instead of two. But the problem was impossible, and of course Descartes never solved it.

There is a milder form of dualism, however, in which at least some human activities—perception, for example—are considered to have both mental and physical properties. This is generally called *property* dualism, though I would prefer the term *aspect* dualism. But Searle wants neither kind and thinks he can avoid them while still defending the distinctness of subjective states from brain states. The pivot for this whole view lies in his repeated assertions that brain states *cause* mental states. Thus he thinks of conscious states as real, physical states in the universe that are caused by brain states, much in the same way as digestion is caused by the activities of the stomach or the fluidity of water is caused by the properties of the individual molecules. Thus he considers that he can avoid a dualistic positing of anything non-physical in the universe, and yet not surrender the distinctiveness of subjective states.

As to their causal connection, Searle says, for instance: "It is just a plain fact about nature that brains *cause* consciousness."[6] I wonder how he thinks he *knows* this. Presumably by recalling that brain

5. Ibid., 211-12.
6. Ibid., 158.

states invariably go together with conscious states. But we saw above that invariable connection does not constitute a proof of *causal* connection. We don't have to be Hume to think of other possibilities. *Is* it "just a plain fact" or rather an *interpretation of* plain facts? I believe that the considerations throughout this essay will point rather to proper brain states as a necessary condition for consciousness, not as its cause.[7]

With this as a prelude, we are ready to begin inquiring into the characteristics of human knowing and, to begin with, of sense perception, always on the lookout for any characteristics that seem, at least, to transcend brain activity.

1.2.2 In sense perception objects are given to us as other than ourselves.

This assertion only makes explicit what you have probably always believed, at least until you were perhaps shaken in this belief by perplexities that have confused the philosophic world for the last 300 years. Our first-hand experience is that we find ourselves confronted with things in a world, extramental bodies that we have to reckon with. As Maurice Merleau-Ponty (1908–1961) put it: "Our perception ends in objects, and the object once constituted, appears as the reason for all the experiences of it which we have had or could have."[8]

Since about the seventeenth century, however, this common sense view, as usually understood, proved fatally vulnerable to difficulties raised against it by such considerable thinkers as Hobbes, Galileo, Newton, Descartes, Locke, and Hume. The upshot of these difficulties, which we shall examine in the next chapter, was that most philosophers since that time have concluded that we are not

---

7. Though I disagree with Searle on several points, I commend to the interested reader his *Mystery of Consciousness* in which he situates and evaluates, from his own perspective of course, the views on brains and consciousness of Francis Crick, Gerald Edelman, Roger Penrose, Daniel Dennett, David Chalmers, and Israel Rosenfield.

8. Maurice Merleau-Ponty, *Phenomenology of Perception*, 67.

experientially confronted with external objects at all, but only with our own private perceptions. We then proceed to suppose that these perceptions *represent* external objects, much as a photograph of a friend represents the friend.

In the next chapter I shall show why this widely accepted "representational" view of perception is both unnecessary and false, and on this promissory note I proceed here to take our apparent experience of extramental objects at face value and suppose that we do indeed perceive *objects in a world*. Then I ask: what must be the structure of that perception?

Everyone, I suppose, will agree that sense perception begins with the stimulation of a sense organ by the action of the external object upon it, followed by an activity of the organ—including its appropriate brain activity—in response to that stimulation. But is that particular brain activity identical with the perception in question, or is the perception, though dependent upon that activity, an activity distinct from the brain activity?

I look up, let us say, and spot the household cat walking into the room. (Make it a dog if you prefer.) I perceive it as an *extramental other*, which is, perhaps, meowing for its dinner. Now there is no doubt that appropriate brain activities must be going on in order for me to see and hear the cat. But do they actually constitute the seeing and the hearing? If they do, how do they generate that manifest aspect of *otherness* involved in the perception?

Those who would identify brain activity with perceptual experience say that experience consists just in having that particular brain activity. The approach of *methodological materialism,* for instance, advocated by Paul M. Churchland and similar to Dennett's, is clear enough from the following passage:

> The basic idea is that cognitive activities are ultimately just activities of the nervous system; and if one wants to understand the activities of the nervous system, then the best way to gain that understanding is to examine the nervous system itself. . . .

The conviction of methodological materialism is that if we set about to understand the physical, chemical, electrical, and development behavior of neurons, and especially of systems of neurons, and the ways in which they exert control over one another and over behavior, then we will be on our way toward understanding everything there is to know about natural intelligence.[9]

But my brain activity is precisely a physical activity taking place within the spatial confines of my own brain. If perception were nothing other than that activity, how could it reveal to me an external object *as external and other,* as outside myself and standing over against myself? There is a vector quality to sense perception that defies interpretation in terms of pure, localized brain activity.[10]

1.2.3 In perception, objects give themselves as *value-laden*, as bearing *importance*.

This is why we pay attention to the traffic before crossing a street: the moving objects about us bear an element of danger. To portray sense perception in the usual way, as simply a display of sense qualities that are value-neutral, bearing within themselves no importance, is simply to ignore an essential element of our everyday experience.

What I am claiming here is that this dimension of importance forms part of the fabric of experience as we *find* it, not as we interpret it after we have already had the sense experience. Otherwise what are we to make of animal instinct? As was noted even in the time of Aristotle, the newborn sheep flees the wolf that it sees or smells even though it has never seen or smelled a wolf before. The element of *danger to be avoided* forms part of the

---

9. Churchland, *Matter and Consciousness*, 96-97.

10. This vector quality of knowing is called its "intentional" aspect, from the Latin *intendere,* to stretch in a particular direction, to aim at something.

immediate sensory experience of the sheep. Yet it can hardly have been acquired, as Hume might have it, by repeated unpleasant experiences with wolves. The first such experience would have been the last. Yet the sense of danger *is* given in the experience just as much as color is.

That the aspect of importance, good or bad, forms part of sense experience itself usually goes unrecognized and that is partly due to its all-pervasiveness. Alfred North Whitehead (1861–1947) noted that we ordinarily recognize things by reason of their differences. Sometimes, he said, we see an elephant and sometimes we don't, so that an elephant when present gets noticed. But the value-dimension of sense perception is always present, so that it is hard to recognize.

Perhaps the clearest example of the value-dimension included within sensation lies in color vision. If you are not completely color-blind—and I apologize to any reader who is—consider what amount of money you would accept in exchange for spending the rest of your life seeing the world only in shades of gray. Would a million dollars be enough? Two million? What this bizarre conception illustrates is the immense *value* that we *feel* in the color-aspect of our vision. When we are looking around us at all sorts of ordinary objects, including flowers and sunsets, we are aware that our experience of colors is of incalculable value to us, value that we would not willingly part with.

Most philosophers after David Hume (1711–1776) would interpret our feeling of value or importance as a purely subjective reaction to a value-neutral display of color impressions. For such philosophers, sensation consists merely of this sterile display, and then we mentally impose upon the display our own subjective reactions to it. We read back into our perception value feelings that do not in fact belong to it.

Whitehead, on the other hand, claims that this interpretation flies in the face of fact; it distorts what we actually experience. The dimension of importance, more or less, and positive or negative, is part of sense experience itself and needs to be accounted for. He shows how we can make rational sense of accepting as authentic our feelings of the value-dimension of sense experience.[11] This is not the place to lay out Whitehead's analysis, though I shall do some of that in the next chapter, but since I judge it to be convincingly in agreement with what I find in my own immediate sense experience, I accept the *feeling of value* as a given aspect of that experience, and I do not see how it could possibly be accounted for simply as localized brain activity.

At the risk of seeming too repetitious, I emphasize once again that I am not here speaking of an emotional feeling that I subjectively attach to my sense impressions. I am not talking about emotion at all, for emotion already connotes subjective reaction. I am attempting to point to a perceptual sense of *value out there,* in the sense of value in what is being perceived. It gives itself to me as part and parcel of my sense experience, and it gives itself as presumably objective and authentic. This is "feeling" in a very special sense of the word. It is a sensible grasping of something, a grasping that is not at all like sensing a color.

More significant instances of this immediate perception of value lie in our grasp of aesthetic beauty and of moral worth. We apprehend a landscape or a great work of art as beautiful, and we feel the worth of friendship. The value of friendship is included in the experience itself, not tacked on later. Once again, I find it incredible that the experience of beauty or of friendship could be simply identified with the brain process that accompanies it. (Dennett would call this a relapse into "folk psychology.")

Now it is always possible to say, "Well, it just *is* brain activity even if it doesn't *feel* like it," and I have no knockdown argument against this bald assertion. But I don't believe it and I wonder whether you do. Such a reductionist explanation just does not match experience. I can't believe that feeling value as value is explainable as a purely neurological brain process. It seems to me that the feelings of otherness as such and of value as such belong to a level of activity that transcends a material activity analyzable in the

---

11. See, for instance, Whitehead's *Modes of Thought,* Lecture Six.

value-neutral terms of science. If that be the case, then the activity of perceiving encompasses within itself, and functionally depends upon, brain activity but is not identified with it. It is a different *kind* of concomitant activity, so sensing is more than brain-related activity of the sense organs.

1.2.4 Another aspect of the value dimension of perception is its sensitivity to possible *goals for action*.

In all our conscious activity we undeniably aim at goals. These goals are *grasped possibilities for value achievement* in the immediate or more remote future. As Aristotle pointed out, everyone desires happiness, either to achieve it or to continue possessing it once achieved. That is the lure toward which all our deliberate activity is directed.

So we not only perceive the value dimension of present objects, we also find ourselves attracted by—hence feel the value dimension of—*possibilities for value in the future*. This is a given perceptive activity. Can it be simply a neurological process taking place within the present space-time confines of the brain?

1.2.5 Knowing and perceiving give themselves in experience as bipolar, having both subjective and objective poles.

We have already noticed the objective aspect of perception, namely that it confronts us with extramental objects as such, with things as other to us. Notice that this imports a *subjective* aspect as well: that the objects of perception or knowing are given to *us as perceivers or knowers*. There is a for-us-as-perceivers dimension to the perceiving itself: the perceiving gives itself as *for the sake of* the perceiver. Once again, I find it unbelievable that such an activity is simply identified with neurological activity taking place within the confines of the brain.

There is thus a *subject-object polarity* within the perceptive act, and this polarity is a particular instance of the dimension of *otherness* that we have already noted in perception. For subject and object stand as polar opposites that nevertheless belong to the very essence of perception. It strains belief to suppose that this dimension of perception can be accounted for solely in the terms of brain functioning.

1.2.6 Human knowing is self-reflexive and imparts a kind of self-reflexiveness to human sense perception.

We humans not only know, we also know that we know. In our immediate awareness we are *present to ourselves* in that awareness, and when we perceive we also implicitly know that we are perceiving. Here I am not chiefly talking about making a deliberate (and unusual) effort to reflect upon our own knowing or perceiving, as when we occasionally turn the searchlight of attention back upon our own activity of knowing or perceiving. Such an act is itself extraordinary enough and arguably inexplicable in terms of pure brain activity. But I point to an ever-present aspect of all our human knowing and perceiving: that it gives itself to us as in one way or another self-reflexive. Our knowing is, as it were, wholly present to itself, and that is just what it means to be *aware* of our own knowing and perceiving.

Once again I propose that this self-reflexive aspect of knowing that accompanies perception is not credibly understandable simply in terms of a brain activity that is itself confined to the conditions of space and time. The eye, for instance, cannot see its own seeing, because the physical aspect of seeing would require some other eye (a kind of meta-eye) to do the seeing of its seeing. Yet whether we are perceiving with our senses or knowing with our mind (whatever that may prove to be), our sensing and our knowing are diaphanous to themselves. They are, as it were, self-transparent. But this self-transparency of knowing transcends the intrinsically material conditions of brain activity. The self-awareness inherent in perception reveals a different *sort* of activity than that of a material process.[12]

---

12. Here I have been speaking of what is revealed by introspection. With regard to this alleged irreducibility of introspective acts to brain activity, Churchland remarks: "The argument from introspection is . . . entirely without force, unless we can somehow argue that the faculty of introspection is quite different from all other forms of observation" (*Matter and Consciousness,* 15). Yes indeed, and that is precisely what I *am* arguing.

1.2.7   On hearing a melody

What is more familiar than the experience of hearing music? But thoughtful reflection on this ordinary experience reveals in the most striking way that this experience cannot be simply identified with the brain activity that is involved with it.

What is it to hear a melody? I ask the reader to think for a moment of a favorite melody, running through it and enjoying it. Now a melody is a succession of different notes experienced as a *unity*. The notes are not experienced in isolation from one another, otherwise they would not be a melody at all. But where does this unity exist? Not in the physical world, because in the musical instruments or in the resulting sound waves each note simply disappears with the arrival of the next. Where then does the melody exist as a unity? Only in your own consciousness.

This togetherness of past notes with present ones that is essential to the experience of hearing a melody has precisely the opposite character from that of a physical activity, for in physical activity each present state displaces the past state rather than includes it. Yet in the hearing of a melody there is an all-togetherness, an inclusiveness, in human perception, and I do not see how this obvious fact could be denied. But then the very nature of the activity that is the experience of hearing music cannot be identical with the physical activity that is brain process, for physical process precisely excludes all its previous stages. Something other than physical process is taking place in perceptual experience.

1.2.8   On understanding speech

Well, there *is* something more familiar than hearing music, and that is engaging in conversation. We are constantly expressing ourselves vocally to others and understanding what is being replied to us in turn. But does not our understanding of speech involve the same *inclusiveness of past with present* that we noticed in the hearing of a melody? If the first words of someone's spoken statement were not still present to us at its conclusion we couldn't make sense of what was said. The first words no longer exist in any physical sense, yet they still exist in our understanding. The statement must be present to us *as a whole* if we are to understand it, and we *do* understand. Like the experience of hearing a melody, the act of understanding speech has the characteristic of *including the past within the present* that just doesn't match the characteristics of physical activities in which the present always *excludes* and supplants the past.

Taking all the above characteristics of perceptive knowing into account, I propose that we are entitled to proceed on the assumption that the experiential activity that is knowing is not simply identical with brain process (statement 1.2 above), and hence is a legitimate arena for philosophic investigation. Such experience is radically different from a purely physical process and so cannot be adequately accounted for by neurobiology. We require a *philosophic* analysis of the different forms of knowing. What such an analysis amounts to will further unfold as we proceed, and it will, as I believe, massively reinforce this claim that knowing is more than a purely biological process.

Let us then begin a more detailed exploration of the form of knowing that is sense perception.

QUESTIONS FOR REVIEW AND DISCUSSION

1. What sort of enterprise is traditional philosophy? What are some ways in which it differs from science?

2. What is meant by saying that knowing is distinct from brain activity?

3. What is the meaning and import of "methodological materialism"?

4. Can you think of an example of your own illustrating the difference between a cause and a necessary condition?

5. What is the importance of saying that consciousness has a first-person ontology?

6. How does Searle think he can avoid property dualism?

7. What are three distinctive characteristics of sense objects as we encounter them in the world, and why do these characteristics cast doubt on identifying sense perception with brain activity?

8. What is the meaning and importance of noticing that sense perception is "bipolar"?

9. In just what way is human sense perception "self-reflexive"?

10. Why does the experience of hearing a melody and understanding speech point to perceiving as a different kind of activity from physical changes, such as those in the brain's activity?

chapter 2

ON PERCEIVING REAL OBJECTS

We do not live simply in a world of sounds and fragrances and colors, we live rather in a world of sounding, fragrant, multi-colored *objects.* At least that is our initial impression. Here is how the poet Gerard Manley Hopkins put it:

> Nothing is so beautiful as Spring—
>> When weeds, in wheels, shoot long and lovely and lush;
>> Thrush's eggs look little low heavens, and thrush
> Through the resounding timber does so rinse and wring
> The ear, it strikes like lightnings to hear him sing;
>> The glassy peartree leaves and blooms, they brush
>> The descending blue; that blue is all in a rush
> With richness; . . .[1]

These external objects harbor danger and delight, power and possibilities, and they are what we are almost always concerned with. We take them for granted as making up the world of our lived experience.

That world *presents* itself to us and we do not normally stop to reflect on how this presenting takes place. Because we don't, we tend

---

1. Gerard Manley Hopkins, S.J., *The Poems of Gerard Manley Hopkins,* "Spring," 67.

to assume that the world outside ourselves is itself just as we experience it, with all its colors and sounds and smells. This is what I am calling *the common sense view of the world*. More technically this view is called "naive realism."

2.1   THE MYTH OF THE THEATER

That the world itself is *just as we find it in our perception,* however, is an assumption that won't survive close examination. Have you, for instance, ever been for a moment unable to find your car because when you saw it under the strange lights of a parking lot it was the wrong color? The night-perceived car was of a different color than what you ordinarily see, yet you don't suppose that anything had happened to the paint. It was not the object itself that had changed, it was the perceived-object, the object as found in your perception of it. Consequently most philosophers, beginning with some of the ancient Greeks but most notably since the seventeenth century, have concluded that we find ourselves confronted in perception not with extramental *things* but rather with our own perceptions, variously referred to as *sense impressions, sense data, sensations, sensa,* or *phenomena*. These are admittedly mental, part of our own perceptual process, and they are thought to *represent* to us the external, extramental world. I call this view, that images but not *things* themselves are given us in perception, "the myth of the theater."[2] It thinks of us as placed before an internal, mental screen on which we find various sense images that we then interpret as standing for or *representing* extramental objects. We are thus in the same position as the prisoners in Plato's cave who had never seen anything but shadows on the wall and so took them for reality itself.[3] In what follows I intend to get rid of that myth by showing that it is both useless and false. We must and can find a better way to understand

---

2. I am using this phrase in a different sense than did Francis Bacon who coined it.
3. See book 7 of Plato's *Republic* for the Allegory of the cave.

sense perception, a way that avoids the myth on the one hand and naive realism on the other.

To repeat: according to the myth we do not find ourselves directly confronted with colored, sounding, and fragrant (or smelly) objects, but merely with our own sensations of color, sound, and smell. What we are given is our own sensations; we can only infer to a world behind them.

Thomas Hobbes (1588–1679) believed in the myth but was troubled by it. He called it "*the great deception of sense.*"[4] You find a later and lucid expression of the myth in an early little book by Bertrand Russell (1872–1970). Russell there considers a table and notes that its visual appearance changes as he walks around it or sees it in different lights, yet he does not think that the table itself (the "real table") thereby changes. But if the appearances change while the table itself does not, it seems to follow both that the appearances are not the table, and that appearances alone are what we encounter. As Russell puts it: "Thus it becomes evident that the real table, if there is one, is not the same as what we immediately experience by sight or touch or hearing. The real table, if there is one, is not *immediately* known to us at all, but must be an inference from what is immediately known."[5]

But hundreds of years earlier, at the very dawn of the modern era, the same myth already haunts the views of Galileo (1564–1642)[6] and Newton (1642–1727)[7] among scientists, and of Hobbes, John Locke (1632–1704), René Descartes, David Hume, and indeed of most later philosophers. Locke, for instance, takes the myth for granted but also confesses to the immediate problem that it poses. He writes: "It is evident the mind knows not things immediately, but only by the intervention of the ideas it has of them. Our knowledge therefore is real only so far as there is a *conformity* between our ideas and the reality of things. But what shall be here the criterion?

---

4. See Thomas Hobbes, *Human Nature*, Ch. 11.
5. Bertrand Russell, *The Problems of Philosophy*, 11.
6. See Galileo's essay "The Assayer" in *Discoveries and Opinions of Galileo*, 274.
7. See Isaac Newton, *Opticks*, 124–25.

How shall the mind, when it perceives nothing but its own ideas, know that they agree with things themselves?"[8]

2.2 THE ABSURDITY OF THE MYTH

How indeed? But then it may fairly be asked whether we have to live with this doctrine at all. To begin with, it flies in the face of the interpretation that we tend naturally to give to sense perception. Ordinary people not yet perplexed by philosophy think that they see, feel, smell, and taste apples, not the appearances of apples. They will report that they put on the brakes because they saw a red light, not because they had noticed an impression of a red light.[9]

But the myth would have us lock ourselves within a dream world of appearance while assuring us that the "real" (that is, non-mental, material) world is forever beyond our immediate grasp. Yet if this be a dream, we normally take it for reality, and that is just why Hobbes calls it "the great deception of sense." The myth in effect canonizes Plato's Allegory of the Cave: it sentences us forever to the fate of the prisoners who can view only images of reality, not reality itself, without the possibility of comparing the images to the real.

In addition, this world of appearance is very little like the world of reality that is supposed to lie behind it. According to the myth, all the smells and colors and sounds are entirely within us, not in the world itself, which is a featureless realm of quantified bodies in motion that merely provoke such sensations in us.

8. John Locke, *An Essay Concerning Human Understanding,* Bk. IV, Ch. IV, 2:228. David Hume agrees: "The slightest philosophy," he says, "teaches us, that nothing can ever be present to the mind but an image or perception, and that the senses are only the inlets, through which these images are conveyed, without being able to produce any immediate intercourse between the mind and the object" *An Enquiry Concerning Human Understanding,* Section 12, 137).

9. This holds even though they might also grant that they could not see a red light unless at the same time they had an impression of a red light—which impression, of course, is not an impression of *seeing* a red light.

Another problem with the myth's world of appearance is that the *succession of different sensations* is, so far as we can ever know, entirely arbitrary, as Hume emphasized later in his *Enquiry*. Though our minds are quick to form habits of expecting similar sensations to follow those of the past, as also did Plato's prisoners, there is no intrinsic connection of one sensation to the preceding one. Sense perception, in this view, is simply a display of unconnected impressions succeeding one another with no more necessity of connection than that by which one image follows another in a slide lecture. Each sense datum is self-contained and has no intrinsic pointers to any other.

More than that, the myth takes for granted that no sense datum can contain an intrinsic pointer to an external event that could be supposed to have provoked it. Although Locke simply took for granted that his sensations were evoked by objects in a world around him, Hume claimed that even for those events that we call "cause" and "effect," each is just simply itself and cannot disclose to us anything beyond itself. Consequently we are, and must remain, he thought, altogether ignorant of the supposed causes, if any, of our sensations. For what evidence do we have for assuming the existence of an extramental object that provokes the sensation? Aside from pure habit of mind, it seems that the only such evidence would lie in a clear causal relationship between the sensation and the object. But that, according to Hume, is exactly what we can never have, for the reasons just mentioned. It is easy therefore to see how the myth, in this form at least, puts us immediately on the road either to subjective idealism, like that of George Berkeley (1785–1853) in which all reality is thought to be mental, or to skepticism.[10]

---

10. It seems an historical irony that Galileo and Newton, the great founders of classical modern science with its aim at a purely objective, quantitative description of the world itself apart from the subjective perspective of observers, should at the same time have numbered themselves among the philosophers who affirmed that we never sensibly encounter the objective world at all but only our own private sense impressions provoked by it.

2.3   SYSTEMATIC GROUNDS FOR THE MYTH

If neuroses can sometimes be overcome by discovering their roots within past experience, it may be possible to discredit this myth of the deception of sense by uncovering and severing not necessarily its historical but its systematic roots. By "systematic" roots I mean the underlying pressure of philosophic presuppositions and principles that naturally lead to the myth. To this end I venture the following assertions.

2.3.1   The myth radically misconceives the possibilities for the direct object of perception.

It assumes that we must perceive either the object (or world) itself and as it is in itself, or else our own perceptions of the object. But the assumption that what we perceive is the *thing in itself* will not survive scrutiny, as we have seen, so the myth supposes that we must be perceiving only the *appearance* of the object within ourselves.

To see better how this tacit, either-or assumption operates, go back again to Russell's table. He notices that the mental appearances (sense data) of the table change as he walks around it, while he does not think that the table itself changes. The appearances therefore cannot be identical with the table, and he seems certainly to be experiencing the appearances. Russell cannot therefore admit that he is experiencing the table rather than its appearances.

In this bit of reasoning, seemingly so conclusive, Russell has distinguished between the appearances of the table on the one hand, and the "real" table on the other, and then tacitly assumed that the object of perception must be either the one or the other. Since the "real" table, so conceived, is presumed to be the table in itself,— stable, unchanging, independent of the constant variations in the ongoing act of perceiving—it cannot be the direct object of this shifting perception. So we are left with only the *appearances* of the table.

But this overlooks a third possibility, that the object of perception is *the appearing table*. The appearing table, as I shall use the term, is indeed the real table but not an independent table, a table somehow taken in itself, a non-relational table. The true object of perception is, rather, *the table in relation to the perceiver within the act of perceiving*. It is a relational table, the table that is the immediate object of the perceiver's act of perceiving, and so a table that, as such, necessarily involves the perceiver.

The perceived table, as such, cannot be divorced from the act by which we perceive it. The world actually encountered in the act of perception is bipolar. It bears witness, as we shall see, to its own potential transcendence of the act of being perceived, and it carries an indelible relation to the one perceiving it, since the perceived object is also the actuality of the perceiver.[11]

Thus we have to distinguish the contents not of two but of three concepts: (a) the "real" table, as Russell puts it, a table conceived as independent of the act of perceiving; (b) the pure appearances of the table, which are the provoked mutations of the senses and admittedly proper to the perceiver; and (c) the perceived, appearing, relational table. It was a false dichotomy between the table itself (considered as independent) and the appearances of the table that implicitly forced Russell to conclude that, since the "real" table, so conceived, cannot be immediately perceived, it must be only the appearances of the table that are perceived. But this conclusion systematically overlooks the third possibility, that what is perceived by means of those appearances is precisely *the appearing, relational table*.[12]

2.3.2 The myth presupposes an inadequate conception of causality.

Hume thought it obvious that the events we call "cause" and "effect" are entirely separate from one another. "The effect," he says, "is totally

---

11. This is entirely in agreement with the epistemology of St. Thomas Aquinas and of Aristotle, particularly as found in the latter's *De Anima*, Bk. III, so I make no claim that the view that I here develop is novel. If Aristotle was basically right—that the act of perception is the actualizing of both the perceiver (as such) and the perceived (as such) in their mutual relationship—he still is.

12. The ontological and epistemological status of the relational table will be considered in some detail below.

different from the cause, and consequently can never be discovered in it."[13] This view has ever since been part of the myth. It has been just taken for granted that there can be nothing of the cause in the effect, except in our own anticipations that a similar event will follow upon familiar and similar antecedents. This aspect of the myth is usually thought too obvious to merit discussing. Yet it is not an evident fact that it must be so, and the price we pay for supposing it to be so is to lock ourselves within the dream-world of appearance postulated by the myth.

For it is usually presupposed by those under the sway of the myth that the external world itself acts upon us through our senses in such a way as to produce particular sense data within us that we then take to be *representative,* more or less, of the external world. The sense data that we do experience *represent* to us a "real" (material) world that we do not experience, and so the myth involves a "representational" theory of perception.

Yet if Hume is right about causality, there is no known or knowable intrinsic relation between the sense datum that we call "effect" and anything in an external world (if there is one) that may be its "cause." Thus even the *representative* relation of appearance to reality cannot be maintained with any assurance. For with Hume's denial of causal connection there is nothing to take us past bare appearances except a naive hope, a mere inclination to think, that on the other side of appearance lies a reality that provokes the appearance within us. Hume himself was not happy about having so little assurance of the existence of anything beyond appearance, and he contented himself with practice rather than theory. "Nature will always maintain her rights," he observed, "and prevail in the end over any abstract reasoning whatsoever."[14]

But Hume's separatist notion of cause and effect is not an obvious truth. Aristotle (384–322 B.C.) maintained that *the activity of the cause is in the effect* and not distinct from it. The mover and the moved, he says, form a single actuality: "There is a single actuality

---

13. Hume, *Enquiry,* Sect. IV, Part I, 29.
14. Ibid., Sect. V, Part I, 41.

of both alike, just as one to two and two to one are the same interval, and the steep ascent and the steep descent are one—for these are one and the same, although they can be described in different ways. So it is with the mover and the moved." And a few lines later he added: "It is *not* absurd that the actualization of one thing should be in another. Teaching is the activity of a person who can teach, yet the operation is performed *on* some patient—it is not cut adrift from a subject, but is of *A* on *B*."[15]

This Aristotelian notion of efficient causality assumes the intrinsic connection of the cause and the effect within the causal act. If, however, you break this intrinsic connection between the causal, external world and its effect on the human senses, then you immediately transform the person from a perceiver to an internal viewer; from someone who perceives a world related to him- or herself in and through the act of perceiving, to someone who views only a display of appearances little different from the images on a movie screen or the shadows on the wall of Plato's cave.

Hume's arbitrary and systematic exclusion of the cause from the very effect that it produces also prevented him from recognizing how this causal connectedness gives itself to us immediately within perception. Thus we have a third factor contributing to the myth, as follows.

2.3.3 The myth also involves an inadequate recognition of the causal dimension included within sense experience.

In examining the origin of the idea of causal influence, Hume invites us to consider one billiard ball colliding with another, and then asks whether we discover within our experience any sensation of the *influence* exerted by the first ball on the second.[16] He makes a convincing case that we do not, and hence consigns the origin of the idea of causal influence solely to the tendency of our mind to expect one usual thing after another.

15. Aristotle, *Physics,* Bk. III, Ch. 3, 202a18–22 and 202b5–7.
16. Hume, *Enquiry,* Sect. IV, Part I, 29; Sect. VII, Part I, 63.

But Hume chose the wrong kind of example with which to rule out the experience of causal influence. He was right to claim that what goes on between two billiard balls forms no part of our own sense experience, but there is plenty of reason to think that if you were struck in the head by one of those balls you would directly and immediately *feel influenced by* it. Later in this chapter we shall examine in some detail this kind of direct perception of causality.

2.4 RELATIONAL REALISM

Where then does this leave us? I think that when we have exorcized the above errors underlying the myth, we find ourselves in a position of *relational realism*.[17] By "realism" I mean a theory of perception that holds not only that there is an external world but that the things in the external world form the direct and normal objects of our perceiving. Let me illustrate this by returning one last time to Russell's table.

Russell thought he could not actually perceive the "real" table since he supposed that the real table leads an independent, impassive existence insulated from the vicissitudes of the conditions of perception. So conceived, the table would be self-enclosed and self-contained, an unrelated table. It would therefore be quite impossible to *perceive* such a table. The only alternative object of perception, to Russell's mind, is pure appearance.

In fact, however, Russell was perceiving a *related table,* an *appearing table,* the table precisely as related to him in his own act of perceiving it. The experienced table is necessarily a related table, not a purely independent table. And of course the experienced table, the appearing table, varies under changing circumstances such as lighting or the perspective of the viewer.

---

17. The phrase "relational realism" is exactly apt but not novel. It was already used by W. Norris Clarke, S.J., in his essay, "Action as the Self-Revelation of Being: A Central Theme in the Thought of St. Thomas," 76.

The appearing table is thus a relational table such that the relationship necessarily includes the perceiver. True, there could be no appearing table without appearances of the table in the perceiver. Nevertheless the appearances of the table are not themselves the table but only the *medium by which* the extramental table is present to the perceiver.

Here is an analogy. Only with the aid of corrective lenses do some people see the world clearly. But in thus seeing things clearly they are *not* looking at their lenses; they are looking at the world *through* their lenses. The lenses serve as a *medium by or through which* they see, not in the manner of a motion picture screen *on* which you see the projected appearances of a world. The lenses are thus not a medium in which but a medium by which or through which you see. According to the myth, however, the sensations or sense-data provoked in us by the external world do not function as a medium through which the world appears to us, but only as a medium *in* which it does, for sense perception is supposed to terminate in the appearances, even as it does at the images on the motion picture screen. Sense perception itself, on this theory, is barred from proceeding farther. Only by shaky intellectual inference do we form any opinions as to what may lie beyond that screen.[18]

18. How difficult it is to break out of representational epistemology, even when one is trying to do so, may perhaps be seen in Roderick Chisholm's *Theory of Knowledge.* In a section entitled "Being Appeared To" he writes:

If you perceive that there is a tree before you, then you believe that your perceptual experience is an experience of a tree—or, in our terminology, you think you are appeared to by a tree. It would be misleading to call the appearance the "*object*" of perception. But it would be accurate to say that, it is *by means of* what you know about the appearance, that you apprehend the object of perception. The philosophical problem of perceptual evidence turns on this question: how is it possible for appearances to provide us with information about the things of which they *are* appearances?

. . . The appearances that we sense are a function, not only of the nature of the things we perceive, but also of the conditions under which we perceive those things. (41–42; italics in the original.)

To further articulate the opposing view of relational realism, I propose the following alternatives to the erroneous presuppositions underlying the myth.

2.4.1 Through sense perception we immediately encounter not sense data but an external world.

Common sense is right about this, as against the extreme views of the myth on the one hand and Berkeley's idealism on the other. It is objects in that extramental, material world that we normally confront in our acts of sense perception.

There is, however, a currently fashionable variant of this, a different way of putting it, that, I am afraid, amounts to a denial of 2.4.1. It is simply to suppose, in the tradition of analyzing language rather than things, that the object of a perception is a *proposition*. Notice how Chisholm wrote (in note 18 above), "If you perceive *that there is a tree before you,* then you believe that your perceptual experience is an experience of a tree" (my emphasis).

2.4.2 The world encountered in perception, however, and *as* encountered in perception, is not an independent world, a world in itself.

Galileo and the others were right about this. A world in itself would be a non-relational world, hence a world that could not enter into that relationship with our own sense powers that makes perception possible.

Objects intrude themselves upon us in sense perception as making a difference to us, as part of the environment that affects us

---

Chisholm rightly says that the appearance is not the object of perception and also that it is a kind of *means by which* we know the tree. Yet he seems to revert to representationalism after all when he supposes that appearance functions as a means only by reason of what we *know about* the appearance. Does that not imply that we first experience the appearance and then *reason from it* to the object? But that is just representationalism all over again. This seems confirmed when he then speaks of "the appearances that we *sense.*" Once again he has us sensing the *appearances* rather than the things.

and that we must deal with. They act causally on our sense organs and thereby make themselves ontologically present to us since, as Aristotle said, the actualization of one entity (the cause) is *in* the other (the effect).

More than that, in virtue of the natural function of the sense organs such sense objects are at the same time *intentionally* present to us (in the root meaning of the term) in virtue of that activity. That is, by nature we *aim ourselves at them* exactly as at the proper objects of our senses.

Furthermore, in acting on us causally in perception, sense objects thereby *reveal themselves as independently capable of activity,* and thus as in themselves transcendent of their activity on us and of our perception of them. If they had no independent existence they would not be able to act upon us. Yet we do not *perceive* them in their independence but rather in their relatedness to us. They make themselves present to us precisely through their activity on us, while that same activity reveals their own ontological independence of their being perceived by us.[19]

Such independence, however, need not imply a denial of the object's intrinsic relatedness to other things apart from its involvement in our act of perception. In other words, you don't have to take this independence to mean that Bertrand Russell was right in his early surmise that "the universe is exactly like a heap of shot,"[20] rather than like the parts of an organism.

If you are acquainted with the philosophy of Immanuel Kant (1724–1804), the above notion of a table existing in its own right, independently of our perception of it though never *perceived* that way, invites a comparison with Kant's doctrine of the "thing in itself," the *Ding an sich.* (If Kant is a stranger to you, you may wish to skip the next two paragraphs.)

In what ways is the above concept of an independent, unperceived table like, and in what ways unlike, Kant's noumenal "thing in itself"? The real and independent table has affinities to Kant's

19. This point will be further elaborated below.
20. Bertrand Russell, *Portraits from Memory and Other Essays,* 39.

"thing in itself" insofar as neither is encountered *as such* in sense perception. The only table we can perceive is a relational table, a table acting causally on our sense organs in such a way as to stimulate their appropriate responses, with the result that it is the causally active (hence related) table that we directly apprehend in sensation. It is not only physically, it is even logically impossible that we perceive a table just as it is in itself—that is, as an utterly unrelated, wholly self-contained table.

On the other hand, the independent table of which I have spoken is nonetheless a spatial object, and that of course cannot be said of Kant's *Ding an sich*. For according to Kant, space itself, as a form of sensibility, is contributed to the experienced object by the mind. Kant's "thing in itself," which is never experienced, cannot itself be spatial. But a non-spatial table is a contradiction in terms. The thing-in-itself, because it is not spatial, cannot possibly be a table or any other object of perception.

2.4.3   The world we encounter in perception is the appearing world, a relational world.

The appearing world, as has been said, is a relational world involving both the external world and ourselves in the act of perceiving. Berkeley was right about this insofar as he claimed that the sensed world is none other than the real world. He was wrong in further claiming that the sensed world is only mental.

But what about hallucinations? Don't they prove that sense data rather than external bodies are the immediate objects of perception? And so don't they refute relational realism and verify the representational theory of perception?

No they don't. In the first place, the very fact that they are abnormal, deceptive, perhaps even pathological, means that they should not be made the paradigm for a theory of perception. Secondly, hallucinations exemplify rather than form an exception to the causal relationships described above. During an hallucinatory experience I may indeed find myself influenced by extramental causes—drugs for instance—and it is not very surprising that diverse causes might sometimes produce similar physiological effects on the perceptual organs, so that I misinterpret the nature of the cause that is acting on me. (The epistemological analysis here may not be very different from that of the oar that appears bent in the water.)

We may accept, then, that ordinarily the appearing world is just that colored, noisy, smelly world we have always supposed it to be. The so-called secondary qualities, such as color and sound, do really belong to the encountered world, though they do not belong to a world in itself, because a world in itself is never what we encounter in our perceiving. Neither are they only appearances in our own minds (at least not usually). I perceive a *red apple,* not a sensation of red that I inferentially attribute to an extended something or other presumably causative of my sensation and which I call an apple. The appearing apple, rather, is a physical, external apple, yet an apple with which I am intimately involved within the relational act of perceiving. This leads to two more conclusions, as follows.

2.4.4   The appearing world is a relational world, and is not mere appearances.

2.4.5   The appearing world is a unity of the external world and the perceiver, for it is the actualization of both in the perceptual order.[21]

I began this chapter with a fragment of a poem that stresses the vividness of the world we sense. In another poem the same poet, Gerard Manley Hopkins, puzzles over how sense perception seems to be at once subjective and objective:

> It was a hard thing to undo this knot.
> The rainbow shines, but only in the thought
> Of him that looks. Yet not in that alone,
> For who makes rainbows by invention?

---

21. This point too will be further explained below.

> And many standing round a waterfall
> See one bow each, yet not the same to all,
> But each a hand's breadth further than the next.
> The sun on falling waters writes the text
> Which yet is in the eye or in the thought.
> It was a hard thing to undo this knot.[22]

If you adopt the view of relational realism that I have proposed above, you can undo the knot that puzzled Hopkins. For no one sees a rainbow-in-itself but always a relational rainbow, a bow that is indeed sunlight as refracted and reflected by countless water droplets, but that is present to each observer solely through its presence in that observer's perceptual activity.

The peculiar, visionary nature of a rainbow accentuates its exclusiveness to a particular observer, yet even the waterfall itself is "not the same to all." For (as we shall see below) there is an authentic sense in which no two observers *see* the same waterfall although they both can be said to be *looking at* the same waterfall. For the seen-waterfall can only be the waterfall as it stands in its relation to a particular observer within the observer's own act of perception. In that sense, then, there are as many perceived waterfalls as there are observers.

But is this theory of relational realism merely fantasy? We need, in the next chapter, to examine more carefully its philosophic foundations so that we know we are on solid ground for all that comes later.

QUESTIONS FOR REVIEW AND DISCUSSION

1. What is here meant by "the myth of the theater"? What is its importance?

2. Can you give an apparently strong argument in favor of the representational view of perception?

---

22. Hopkins, *The Poems of Gerard Manley Hopkins,* 129–30.

3. What does Hobbes mean by "the great deception of sense," and why does he think it is unavoidable?

4. What does one's conception of causality, or the lack of it, have to do with the myth of the theater? Where do you find the activity of an "efficient" cause?

5. Why does the myth put us on the road to either idealism or skepticism?

6. From his observation of a table, how does Russell argue to representationalism?

7. How do you make sense of a third possibility besides a *thing in itself* and *the appearance of a thing?*

8. How does causal influence show up in our immediate experience?

9. What is meant here by "relational realism"? Why both terms?

10. In what sense does a sense datum constitute a *medium by which* objects are perceived?

11. How does that differ from a sense datum regarded as a *medium in which?*

12. What does it mean to say that external objects are "intentionally" present to us?

13. How do you know that sense objects have an extramental reality of their own?

14. What does the concept of the world as "like a heap of shot" have to do with causality?

15. Why don't hallucinations prove that representational epistemology is correct?

16. Do you think relational realism unties Hopkins's "knot"? Why or why not?

chapter 3

FOUNDATIONS OF RELATIONAL REALISM

W*hat are the philosophic foundations required to support the* theory of relational realism I have just sketched? Here we need to do some philosophical digging just to identify these foundations. We don't need to work them out fully—that would require a whole metaphysics—but only to point toward them. In doing this I introduce a few technical terms for the sake of precision.

3.1 FUNDAMENTAL AND APPARENT PERCEPTION

A first foundation for relational realism lies in an aspect or mode of perception that is quite different from that mode of perception that philosophers normally pay attention to, which is a basically passive display of colors, sounds, and so forth. In order to identify the other, richer dimension of perception that I have in mind, let me put it into the context of some conclusions we have already reached.

We have noticed that it is easy to make the mistake of thinking that what we perceive is our own impressions rather than objects. Of course the impressions are indispensable for the perception of objects, since we necessarily perceive the objects *through* these impressions, but we have to ask more exactly how this happens.

When analyzing sense perception philosophers have almost always fixed their attention on the clean-cut impressions of sight or sound: on a display of color or sound images. Such impressions are just what Hume was thinking of when he rightly pointed out that they contain no intrinsic relations to each other or to anything else. They just are what they are, like images projected on a screen, and so can't possibly point to anything beside themselves. But because colors, sounds, and smells are relatively clear and definite, they are also easiest for our analytic minds to deal with, and we tend to suppose that they make up the whole of perception.

But is there any reason to expect that what is most fundamental in sense perception is just what is most clear and sharply defined? Why might not the more fundamental be the more vague instead? Earlier, when considering the systematic grounds for the myth of the theater, I suggested that an inadequate recognition of the causal dimension included within sense experience was one of the factors contributing to the origin of the myth. Pursuing this same point, I now call attention to an essential aspect of sense perception that simply cannot be described in terms of the entertainment of qualities such as colors and sound. This aspect of perception was first clearly pointed out by Whitehead, who called it "perception in the mode of causal efficacy." By that abstract but accurate phrase he meant to say that our perceptual experience consists in encountering objects not only through the reception of their qualities, such as color, but by *our feeling their influence upon us and their importance to us.*[1] In what follows I shall call this deeper mode of perception *fundamental perception.*[2]

---

1. Whitehead deals with this topic in his principal book, *Process and Reality*, Part II, section viii, and in *Symbolism,* Ch. II.

2. Whitehead is not alone in stressing this causal aspect of perception. John Searle, whose acquaintance we have already made, also affirms this causal dimension of sense perception. He writes: "On my account the visual experience does not represent the causal relation as something existing independently of the experience, but rather part of the experience is the experience of being caused" (*Intentionality,* 74). And later in the same book he writes: "I get a direct experience of causation from the fact that part of the Intentional content of my experience of perceiving is caused by the object perceived, i.e., it is satisfied only if it is caused by the presence and features of the object" (ibid., 130).

Whitehead contrasted fundamental perception with the display-like entertainment of sense qualities such as colors and sounds, and he called this latter, "perception in the mode of presentational immediacy." I shall hereafter call it, more simply, *apparent perception.* Hume was considering only apparent perception when he asked if he had any sense impression of causal *influence* and had to reply that he did not. No color or sound of itself reveals anything beyond itself, hence certainly not the *causal influence* of something other than itself. All Hume could find was the feeling of the habit of his own mind, formed through past experience, of expecting that the future would once again be like the past. As he tellingly remarked, if in observing one billiard ball collide with another you claim that you *see* the influence of the first on the second, that influence must be a color; if you claim you *hear* it, that influence must be a sound; and so on. To avoid these absurdities Hume concluded that causal influence is not *perceived* at all, except insofar as you feel the tendency of your own mind to go from one perception to another.

But what is this fundamental perception that Whitehead claims is an intrinsic aspect of our total perceptual experience? He points to the experience of a man who has been sitting in a dark room and who blinks when the lights are suddenly turned on. If you ask him why he blinked, he will tell you, "The light made me blink," and if you ask him how he knows that, he will say that he knows it because he *felt* it. Whitehead takes the man at his word; the compulsion to blink is just what the man did feel.[3] Let us too admit that fact and try to understand it.

We noted above that Hume had rightly failed to find any sense impression of the causal influence of one billiard ball upon another, but he was looking for it in the wrong place. He did not ask himself what his experience would have been if he had been hit in the forehead with one of the balls. Suppose it happened to you. Would you not *sensibly feel* that the ball has affected you? More generally, do you not *feel* that the surrounding world is influencing you right now, that it makes a difference to you?

3. Paraphrased from Whitehead's *Process and Reality,* 174–75.

Besides the feeling of the causal impact of the world upon us, and inextricably linked with it, there are at least two other chief features of experience that are immediately given in fundamental perception. Both are at first hard to notice, partly because they are vague, and partly because they pervade all our perceiving. Since there is no getting away from them, we can't notice them by the method of differences. Yet upon careful reflection they are, I think, undeniably present in perception.

One such feature is the ongoing *feeling of the derivation of the present from the immediate past.* You *feel* the present as issuing from the immediate past and as laying a certain necessity on the immediate future. Your sense experience of the world includes a feeling of its own *vector character in time.* Such a feeling is not given in what I have called apparent perception. For in that mode of perception the various impressions are radically isolated from one another, like the successive images on a motion picture screen. These images are cut off from those that came before and those that follow after by intervals of complete darkness. If you could hold a conversation with such an image and ask it what came before it, or what will come afterward, it could have nothing at all to say. It is blankly ignorant of any past or future.

Yet you do in fact *feel* the present as continuous with and deriving from the past, and that feeling is not describable in terms of the isolated impressions provided by apparent perception. It is a clear instance of fundamental perception.

Another feature of fundamental perception is the *feeling of value or worth.* We already noticed this in the first chapter, particularly in our immediate feeling of the worth of color vision. The value of color vision is immediately given as part of the experience itself; it is *felt,* it is not subjectively *inferred* afterward. So too of other aspects of the given world: its danger or its delight. In acting on us causally the objects of the world also give themselves as freighted with importance, good or bad, and we know this because we feel it. That feeling is a fundamental part of our sense perception.

I can't stress too strongly that the "feelings" in question here are not feelings in the ordinary sense of the word. Whitehead is not talking about feeling cold or feeling frightened or feeling attracted. Those are all subjective feelings. He is talking rather of "feeling" in the sense of *encountering in sense perception an aspect of the world as experienced*. These are, if you will, objective feelings; they put us in touch with the world around us. He claims that they form the more important aspect of sense perception even though it is the aspect that is normally overlooked. I think he is right on this, and I invite you to reflect on your own sense experience and see if it does not include the sense of being acted upon by the world, the sense of importance or value (good or bad), and the sense of the flow of the present from the immediate past, ushering into the immediate future.

Thus one foundation for our theory of relational realism is epistemological. It has to do with our manner of experiencing, and it consists in recognizing fundamental perception by which we literally feel causal influence and importance.

3.2   HOW THE CAUSE IS IN THE EFFECT

The other foundation, however, is metaphysical. We need a theory of cause and effect, unlike that of Hume, in virtue of which it makes sense to say that the cause in its causing is literally in the effect rather than isolated from it.

Now such a theory of causality is already at hand, for instance in the metaphysics of Aristotle and of Thomas Aquinas, as well as in Whitehead's theory of "prehensions."[4] There is no need here to work out any such theory in detail. Roughly, however, it amounts to acknowledging that when we accidentally touch a hot coil on the stove, the coil is, unfortunately, right now acting on us by its heat. It is the coil's activity that we are feeling. Aristotle gave the example of teaching and learning: that the teaching of the teacher is the selfsame activity as the learning of the learner, but viewed

---

4. In Whitehead's metaphysics one actual entity is not only felt by another as causally influential upon it, it is an intrinsic constituent of the very identity of the entity feeling it.

from a different perspective—an instance of the presence of the cause in its effect. In a similar way, *we feel the external object as present to us* precisely in feeling its activity upon our senses.

To grasp this more clearly it may help to notice how such a view of causal presence contrasts with the more common view of causality that has been prevalent since the seventeenth century. Then, and now, we are accustomed to think of cause and effect as of two different events, or states of affairs, at two different times, such that, given the first state, or "cause," the second state, or "effect," always, or most always, or even inevitably, follows. (The exact relation of the first state to the second is just the controversial point.)

Now it is evident that if this were a complete or satisfactory account of the relation of cause and effect, it would never be possible to claim, as I have above, that the activity of the cause is literally *in* the effect, because on the above conception, the state of affairs that is the cause is regarded as entirely separate from the state of affairs that is the effect, as Hume claimed. But there is every reason to believe that this concept of causality is inadequate as a tool of philosophical analysis.

For one thing, it simply fails to do justice to what we actually experience—namely that we do *feel* the causal activity of external objects as they act upon us. If that concept of causality can't make sense of this experience, so much the worse for the concept.

For another thing, this conception of the relation between cause and effect proves to be self-contradictory with regard to *time*, and so it can't be adequate. To see this, reflect again on what it says. It regards the "cause" as the total state of affairs, given which, the "effect" follows at a later time. But is this concept not self-contradictory? Why does the effect follow only *later,* if the cause already contains everything needed to produce the effect? What accounts for the time delay if there is nothing left to add? *Something* must be going on, something must be being added to what was present with the cause, if the instant at which the effect comes into being must be later than the instant at which the cause is given. Yet the state of affairs called the cause was supposed to be already complete. Why then is the effect not *simultaneous* with the cause rather than later? But if simultaneous, would that not be open to the idea that the causality of the cause is *in* its effect rather than separate from it?

So we have to develop, or adopt, a conception of causality that allows us to make sense of the cause as efficaciously present within its effect. As I remarked above, both Thomas Aquinas's metaphysics and that of Whitehead already embody such conceptions, and so could serve to found a theory of relational realism such as I have described above.

3.3   HOW THE PERCEIVER "BECOMES" THE PERCEIVED

Along with understanding the activity by which the object makes itself present to the perceiver through its own causal activity, we need a theory outlining how the perceiver, in virtue of the object's causality upon it, exercises its own proper activity of *perceiving*. By this activity the perceiver, in a unique way but literally, *becomes the perceived*.[5] Once again, such theories of intentional activity are at hand, at least in the philosophies of Aquinas and of Whitehead. Let me roughly sketch how Aquinas (1225–1274) understands this (though adapting it to modern knowledge of the brain), for his is the simpler theory.

By its causal activity upon you the perceiver, the object impresses something of itself—some distinctive *character* (Thomas calls it a "form")—upon your sense organs and ultimately upon your brain. In virtue of that character received in your senses and your brain, your brain responds—or more exactly, you respond through your brain—with a perceptive activity that embodies the character in question. Now, every activity is an activity in *existing,* and since the above activity of perceiving has the character or form of the object at which it aims, then by this activity you *are* the object, though in the order of *perceiving* (in the "intentional" order). Thus the act

---

5. Such an activity is called "intentional," not in the sense of purposeful but in the sense that the perceiver's activity directs itself toward, aims at, the perceived.

of perceiving naturally incorporates within itself both you the perceiver and the object perceived. *Thus perceiving is the actuality of both you the perceiver and of the object perceived.*

This only makes sense if you grant that perceiving is a radically different *sort* of activity from simple brain activity. And that, as we have seen, is just where the evidence points. And if you do grant that, it is easy to see how this oneness of the perceiver and the perceived within the act of perception exactly fits the theory of relational realism advanced above. For it is solely within this perceptual act that the object can give itself to and be attained by you the perceiver, and within this perceptual act the object is necessarily and dynamically relational, not an object-in-itself but an object-for-you-the-perceiver.

3.4   THE INDEPENDENCE OF THE OBJECT

There is an essential point that needs to be further elaborated before we go any farther. I have argued that the object encountered in sense perception is not the object as it is in itself but the object as it stands related to the perceiver within the act of perception. But if it is not the object in itself, how does relational realism avoid a kind of Berkeleian idealism? For Berkeley, *to be* means exactly *to be perceived* (or to perceive), so that there is no reality to the object perceived other than its status exactly as perceived. Doesn't relational realism, like Berkeley's idealism, deny to the object its own independent existence, existence in its own right?

No it doesn't and the reason was already sketched in chapter two. We have noticed that the object is immediately *felt as affecting our sense organs.* That is what it means for us to experience the object as giving itself to us in perception. But then the object is felt as *causally operative* on us. We distinguish real objects from imaginary ones precisely by this feeling of being *acted upon* by real objects.

Now to be able to act causally, to affect us, belongs only to things that exist somehow in their own right. I can't of course *demonstrate* this, not because it is not true but because it is evident. But if objects *act* on me by provoking my sense organs, they at the same time reveal themselves as existing independently of my mind.

Suppose I consider something so ordinary as the tree I am looking at. I have argued, successfully I hope, that I find myself confronted with the perceived-tree, the tree as related to me in the act of perception, not the tree just in itself. A tree wholly unrelated to me would also be simply unknown to me and it might as well not exist at all so far as I could ever know.

So although the tree precisely as perceived by me is the relational tree, it is nevertheless the *real* tree. It is not a figment of my imagination or perception. I do perceive the real tree, but the real tree precisely as standing in the perceptual relation to me. (A "real tree," in other words, is not synonymous with a "tree in itself.") The real tree is causally acting upon me, otherwise I should not see it at all, and hence I already know that it is capable of existing and acting in its own right. It is independent or autonomous in its own existence, even though I can never possibly perceive it just as it is in itself. I can't, as it were, catch it in the act of being just itself, though I can and do know that it does exist and act in itself apart from my perceiving it. Relational realism, therefore, is not troubled by Berkeley's perplexity about what happens to the tree when I am no longer perceiving it, nor does it require God to keep the tree in existence in the absence of any created observers.

3.5 LOOKING BACK

In this admittedly sketchy account of the objectivity of sense perception I have nevertheless tried to establish the plausibility of the following conclusions.

3.5.1 In sense perception we encounter real objects in a world, not just our own sense impressions. The objects, however, give themselves to us through, or by means of, our sense impressions. Common sense is right about this point, and I therefore reject the representational view of perception, what I have called the myth of the theater.

3.5.2 These objects, however, as encountered in perception, are not objects just as they are in themselves but objects as related to us within the act of perceiving. Common sense is wrong about this, and this error led to the myth of the theater.

3.5.3 There is an essential aspect of sense perception by which we immediately feel the causal influence upon us of the objects in the world and of their worth to us, good or bad. This aspect of perception, usually overlooked, I have called "fundamental perception." Recognition of this intrinsically evident mode of perception enables us to make sense of our first conclusion, that objects, not sense impressions, are what we encounter in perception.

3.5.4 It is possible to make metaphysical sense out of how the object can thus give itself to us in perception, and further, how in perceiving we in a sense become the perceived object.

3.5.5 Thus the realistic or objective aspect of perception is authentic and rationally respectable. We have excellent grounds for affirming that the sunset really is red and roses fragrant without at the same time being in peril of the kind of mentalism that Berkeley thought was the only alternative to the myth. For the world that we sensibly perceive is indeed the real, material world, but it is *perceived as* relational, as related to us in our very act of perceiving. And although the world gives itself to us precisely as our own world, we do not thereby deprive it of its own pole of transcendence. We can legitimately affirm that it exists on its own, apart from our perceptions of it. There is therefore no reason to remain captive to the myth that tells us sense perception is a deception and that we can never escape from the theater or from Plato's cave.

QUESTIONS FOR REVIEW AND DISCUSSION

1. How does "fundamental perception" differ from "apparent perception"? Why can't causal influence be revealed in apparent perception?

2. What are three different aspects of experience given in fundamental perception?

3. In what sense can the (efficient) cause be in its effect? Make up some examples.

4. Why does the usual notion that the effect must come later than the cause involve an incoherence, so that something must be wrong with it?

5. In what sense does the perceiver become the perceived, and how does this fit the theory of relational realism?

6. How does relational realism avoid becoming an idealism, like that of Berkeley, for whom "to be" is the same as "to be perceived"?

chapter 4

THE REMARKABLE STRUCTURE
OF PERCEIVING

In this chapter we try to uncover some of the chief characteristics of sense perceiving. I shall describe perceiving as we find it, as we live it. And since all our conscious experience is grounded in sense perception, I shall be trying to describe the foundation of all our conscious life.

In this undertaking I shall assume that your experience is fundamentally like mine, so I'll sometimes say "I," sometimes "we." Also, the main aim here is *description* of what we actually find, on reflection, to be the case about our sense perceiving.[1] You must ask yourself whether the description fits your own experience. Though the aim here is mainly description, it will naturally suggest something of its own interpretation in the light of what was concluded in the previous chapter.

---

1. In technical terms, this chapter aims to sketch a very simple *phenomenology of perception*—a description of the given structures of perception, though not in the sense of Edmund Husserl (1859–1938), who in a sense divorced the experience of perception from what is perceived. My attempted description is more in the vein of Maurice Merleau-Ponty, for whom the act of perceiving, far from being purely mental, necessarily involves the body. See, for instance, his *Phenomenology of Perception,* especially Part Two: The World as Perceived.

There are special difficulties attendant upon trying to describe perceiving. One is that our attention is usually focused on the objects of perceiving rather than on the perceiving itself. It takes a special effort to shift attention from the objects to the act. A similar difficulty is that we cannot get away from the very act of perceiving so as to view it, as it were, from the outside. None of our conscious experience, of whatever sort, would be possible without some sense perception. Thus we can't isolate it for examination but must catch it redhanded within the perceiving itself. We can only recognize its features by deliberate reflection upon it as it is taking place.

There is also an historical impediment to our exploration of perceiving. It is the tendency, especially since Descartes, to think of perceiving as a purely mental act. I shall on the contrary make no such presupposition, and in fact the description I shall draw will regard perceiving as inextricably involved with bodily functioning. It is no secret, after all, that we see with our eyes and hear with our ears.

With this as prelude, I venture to elaborate upon the following fundamental assertion about what I—and I presume each one of us—finds in our own act of sense perceiving.

4.1   THE SENSED WORLD PRESENTS ITSELF TO ME AS SOMETHING THAT MATTERS.

The sensed world is composed of an indefinite set of *objects,* and for the moment I concentrate my attention on them. I have already argued that it is reasonable to think that objects are indeed what I encounter in perception, not just my own sense impressions of them. These objects *present themselves to me* with a certain irresistible force. They impose themselves on me, and I know this because I *feel* it (recall what was said about "fundamental" perception). I am not free to dismiss them as I can my own imaginings; I have to deal with them.

Explore your own sense perceiving at this very moment. Take your eyes off the book and notice what else you see, hear, and feel. When I myself do that I see palm trees and a rose garden. I feel the chair I am sitting on, I hear a rustling of a breeze in the trees, and

I smell a spring breeze. This is indeed a pleasant experience and I would not want to change it. But even if I did, I couldn't: there they are, the seen and faintly heard trees, the breeze, the scents. I know that these things are not imaginary because they impose themselves on me. Because of this causal imposition, this "making present" to me, they reveal themselves not only as external to me but as independent in their activity, as agents in their own right, and hence as existents in their own right.

They also reveal themselves as *things that matter* to me. That is a phrase I have borrowed from Whitehead, and he deserves to be quoted more fully: "Our enjoyment of actuality is a realization of worth, good or bad. It is a value experience. Its basic expression is—Have a care, here is something that matters! Yes—that is the best phrase—the primary glimmering of consciousness reveals, something that matters."[2]

Don't you find the same? Many or most perceived objects are of trivial importance to us, yet others are literally vital. I know that the importance of any objects to me lies in their relationship to my own aims and projects. All my consciously deliberate behavior is goal-aimed (teleological), and objects either help me or hinder me in reaching my goals. Thus my own life-projects affect the relevance of objects to me, how they matter to *me*. Yet I can't believe that their value, good or bad, reflects *only* my own subjectivity. I may, as an individual, be more or less sensitive to certain values, but those values give themselves to me as *in the things*. And whether the importance of certain things is great or small to me, positive or negative, they in fact give themselves to me not as indifferent but as value-laden. Value is *experienced* as having both a personal ("subjective") and an out-there ("objective") polarity.

And objects, whatever their value dimension, give themselves to *me*. There is a for-me-ness in the way objects present themselves in perceiving. Although the objects of perception give themselves as external and autonomous, as we saw in the previous chapter, nevertheless *as* they give themselves within perception they are ineluctably

---

2. Alfred Norrh Whitehead, *Modes of Thought,* 116.

related to me the perceiver. Despite the misconceptions of ordinary common sense, objects *as perceived* do not give themselves simply as they are in themselves but as they are for me the perceiver.[3]

This is the *subjective pole* of the act of perceiving. I myself am part of the act of perceiving just as much as the objects I perceive, yet in a way different from them, for in perceiving I am not an object but a subject.

I may compare myself in some ways to a camera. There is an evident sense in which (mirrors perhaps excepted) a camera is never in its own photographs. By its very nature it is not an object that it can photograph. Yet in another sense a camera is *always* in its own photographs, even though not as an object. For instance, if there is a defect in its lens, that defect will be found in every picture the camera takes. Indeed, the characteristics of any lens in the camera, better or poorer, are seen in its every photograph. In general, the capacities of the camera, for better or for worse, are embodied in every one of its pictures.

In an analogous way, I never find my *self* (even *with* mirrors) as an object of my sense perceiving. I don't see or hear or touch my perceiving self. Yet I am always within my act of perceiving, not as an object but as a subject, as the one doing the perceiving. My perceiving, after all, is an activity, and precisely an activity of me the perceiver. Hence I find that my perceiving is *bipolar* since it encompasses, though in different ways, both the objects perceived and me the perceiver.[4]

---

3. That this last sentence does not contradict what I said in the previous paragraph about the objectivity, rather than pure subjectivity, of values will be clear if put into the previous context of relational realism, in which it is the *object* that is thus related, but given only *as* related.

4. In perhaps the most notorious case of overlooking this subjective pole of experience, David Hume confesses: "When I enter most intimately into what I call *myself,* I always stumble on some particular perception or other, of heat or cold, light or shade, love or hatred, pain or pleasure. I never can catch *myself* at any time without a perception, and never can observe any thing but the perception." (*A Treatise of Human Nature,* I, iv, vi, 252). But Hume was looking for himself as an object, and of course he failed to find such a self. All the while he kept referring to the subject, the "I," that was doing the searching, yet always failed to notice it.

Returning once again to the objects of my perception, I also notice that I can perceive them only *perspectivally*—from certain limited *perspectives*. If I speak of vision, I must view an object from a certain angle and under certain lighting conditions. There is simply no viewing an object from every possible direction. If there be a God's-eye view of an object that exhausts its capacity to be viewed, it cannot be literally a *view*, and certainly it is not ours. The same must be said of our other senses, of which the most fundamental is touch. The table before me, on which my computer rests, is unlimited in the ways I can encounter it in touch. Every such touch literally puts me in touch with the table, yet none can exhaust it. It can be thought that the very concreteness of objects consists in, or at least is the source of, their inexhaustibility in being perceived.

Here I notice the ease with which I naturally assume that the objects of perception have a certain *stability*. They remain perceptibly identifiable, at least over some period of time, otherwise I would not be able to perceive the same object for more than an instant. This is connected to the object's causal independence as noted above. Yet there is something quite remarkable about an object's character *as perceived,* namely, that it is perceived as *stationary*. When I think more about this I find it quite astonishing, and once again a phenomenon that appears to *defy explanation in purely biological terms.*

What I mean is this. It has been scientifically established that the human eye, even when intently fixed upon some object, does not in fact remain motionless but constantly shifts from one position to another. All the more when I have no particular intention of fixing my gaze on something—let us say I am just walking absentmindedly through a room concerned about some errand. Now certainly in the latter case, and even in the former, my eyes are in very considerable *relative motion* with respect to the objects they see, so that the light falling upon my retinas from any perceived object is constantly shifting from one part of my retinas to another. The "retinal images," if you will, of the object are constantly shifting their positions. Yet my perceptual *experience,* despite all this shifting around on my retinas, is that the object—say the picture on the wall of the room—remains *still,* motionless. It is *perceived* as fixed despite the constantly changing retinal inputs to my brain. Can this be explained in terms of purely biological activity?

There is yet another notable character of perceiving. At the beginning of this description I said that the world is composed of an indefinite set of objects of perception, yet that seemingly obvious remark needs itself to be probed. The world that I encounter in perception does not give itself simply as a sum of objects. It gives itself as a *totality*, a whole, of which both the objects and I myself play an indispensable part. I literally feel myself within a unified whole, though almost always concerned with some particular object or other.

Once again, Whitehead provides an insightful description of this aspect of perception. He says that it is "the vague grasp of reality, dissecting it into a threefold scheme, namely, 'The Whole,' 'That Other,' and 'This-My-Self.' "[5] In fact, in that same lecture Whitehead more than once links this perception of wholeness with the value-dimension of perception. He writes, for instance: "Attention yields a three-fold character to the 'Something that matters'. 'Totality', 'Externality', and 'Internality' are the primary characterizations of 'that which matters.' "[6]

4.2   PERCEIVING IS AN INCLUSIVE ACTIVITY

When I take the above observations of sense perceiving into account, and think of them as a whole, I find their structure remarkable. Sensory perceiving delivers to me not just sensations but a *world*, a world heavy with importance and relevance. The star that is light-years away not only alters my retinas when I look toward it, it gives *itself* to *me*, as standing *out there*, and as bearing *importance*, more or less. There is a real sense in which, when I look at the star, I am out there with it, since, as we saw in the previous

5. Whitehead, *Modes of Thought*, 110.
6. Ibid., 116.

chapter, in my act of perceiving the star and I are united within a single activity. In a special yet literal sense I become it when I see it.

This world-giving aspect of perceiving can hardly be exaggerated. Yet it is correlative to its equally remarkable opposite pole. In the act of perception not only is the world in me, I also am in the world. The experiential—that is, the perceived—world is the only world I have ever known, and I now recognize that it stands inextricably related to me within my act of perceiving. But I also feel myself as related to it, I feel myself as part of that world. The world and I march together, as the French say, within the act which is sense perception.

In this respect Berkeley was at least partly right in his insight that to be *is* to be experienced. For a world to be real to *me* means, first of all, for it to be experienced by me. And for me to be in a world means for me to perceive, to experience that world. And this is the first sense in which I say that perceiving has an inclusive structure: it includes me the perceiver and the perceived world within a single activity.

A second sense in which perceiving is inclusive is that it includes within itself all the requisite activities of the sense organs yet is not simply identified with them. Perceiving is impossible without those activities, but perceiving itself forms a higher, overarching structure within which alone those sense activities find their meaning. Within the act of perceiving, the organic activities of the senses and of the brain find a place in a higher structure. Perceiving, therefore, bears a *different logical structure* from that of organic activity. To try to reduce perceiving to organic activity is, in philosophic jargon, to make a category mistake. It would be like supposing that the process which is university education consists precisely (and only) in the delivery of lectures by professors and the hearing of lectures by students. Of course the giving and hearing of lectures is an integral part of university education as we understand it, but it is not itself the educational process within the minds of the students.

A third sense in which perceiving is inclusive is that, by reason of its very nature, perceiving, as an activity of the perceiver, includes its own past, especially its immediate past, as part of its present. This was already noted in the first chapter where the experience of hearing a melody and of carrying on a conversation was analyzed and found to be incompatible with a purely physical process. For it is characteristic of the motion of bodies in space, for instance, that they can be in only one place at a time. Correlative with that, each "now" of such motion excludes all other nows, all its pasts as well as its futures, just as each place excludes other places. Yet that exclusion is simply not what happens in my hearing a melody or understanding speech. The previous notes of the melody are still included within my experiential "now," otherwise I could not hear a melody at all, and this sort of inclusion of the past within the present cannot describe purely physical activity. The same point is illustrated in any human conversation. If I do not hold within the present of my consciousness the previous words of your spoken sentence, I cannot make any sense out of it when you get to the end. But I do do this, even though the earlier words are physically gone, just as are the previous notes of the melody, and I do it because the earlier parts of the sentence are held within my conscious present. This inclusion of the past within the present is peculiar to perception, or at least to that ongoing consciousness that always accompanies perception, if they be different.

This leads to a fourth and final sense in which one could consider perception to be inclusive. It is, so to speak, inclusive of itself. At least I may perhaps be permitted to use that expression to indicate the self-reflexive aspect of perceiving. As noted in the first chapter, I not only perceive things in a world, I am aware that I perceive them. This awareness or self-reflexiveness accompanying perception is not itself just an additional instance of perception. My awareness that I am seeing something is not an additional case of seeing, and if it were, then there would be required still another seeing for the seeing of the ordinary and so forth, *ad infinitum*.

4.3   A ROUGH PICTURE OF PERCEIVING

This simple description has, I am afraid, barely scratched the surface of the character of sense perceiving, and it has not pretended to say anything particularly original.[7] Yet I think it is accurate as far as it goes. It may help now to summarize some of the more important points that have appeared, both in this chapter and in the previous ones.

4.3.1   Sense perceiving is the dynamic unity, in the intentional order, of both the perceiver and the perceived, wherein the world is in the perceiver and the perceiver in the world.

4.3.2   It is thus bipolar, objective and subjective, and gives itself as such.

4.3.3   The unity of the world and of the perceiver within that world are themselves felt in what I have called fundamental perception.

4.3.4   In perceiving, the world and its objects are felt as important to the perceiver and the perceiver's aims.

4.3.5   Sense perceiving includes its past, or at least its immediate past, within its present.

4.3.6   Human sense perceiving is accompanied by self-awareness, so that it is present to itself in that awareness.

Since none of the above characteristics (4.3.1 to 4.3.6) fits, as it seems to me, the purely organic or biological, space- and time-bound activities of the bodily senses or of the brain, I must draw the following conclusion.

4.3.7   Sense perceiving is a unique kind of activity with a logically different structure than that of organic or brain activity.

---

7. I am sure it is indebted to some of the insights of Edmund Husserl and of Maurice Merleau-Ponty.

Sense perceiving includes and requires the organic activities of the senses and of the brain, but it is distinctly different from them, and it gives them their functional meaning. In its several characteristics it transcends the necessary space-time limitations of purely organic activity.

These additional insights about the unique structure of perceiving, then, give considerable support to the provisional claim made in the first chapter that knowing and even perceiving are activities not wholly explainable in terms of neuronic biology. The biological processes of the senses and of the brain are necessary processes included within the activity of perceiving, but they are not perceiving itself, which is an activity of an altogether different order dependent upon them.

The above reflections shed light on the sort of *world* that gives itself in the act of perceiving. In that act you the perceiver become the perceived (in the sense described above), and you do it precisely through the activities of your sense organs. The world you thus encounter, precisely *as* perceived, is smelly or colorful or noisy, or all those, just insofar as your organs of smelling and seeing and hearing are healthy. Your external senses are your windows to the world.

But as your bodily senses have their strengths, so also they have their natural limitations. We humans, unlike some other living creatures, are restricted in what we can visually see to a band of light-energy that does not include infrared or ultraviolet. We have no imaginative image of what seeing the world through infrared or ultraviolet light would be like. From this obvious reflection, other observations emerge.

The first is a reinforcement of our earlier conclusion that in perceiving, the perceived object, which we in a sense become, is inherently *relational,* ordered to us within the act of perceiving. The world in itself, or objects in themselves, are not what we encounter in perceiving but a world and objects tailored to our own capacities of perceiving them. We do perceive the world and objects, but only from the perspective of our own sense powers. There is indefinitely more to objects than we can perceive with our senses, and exploring this "more" is a principal task of physical science. In the fifth chapter we shall roughly examine how science does this.

The second observation is that our sense powers naturally set up for us a *horizon* of possible perceived worlds. Just as the visible horizon defines the limits of what the sailor can see on the ocean, so the peculiarities and limitations of our sense powers define the limits of the *sorts* of worlds we can naturally perceive. Infrared worlds, for instance, lie beyond that horizon.

This conception of horizons of knowing is, of course, a tool for understanding rather than a matter of direct observation, since we can't see what it is that we don't see—what is beyond our sense horizon—nor can we see our perspective for seeing. Yet the concept helps us become intellectually aware of the limited nature of our knowing.[8]

There can be many horizons, and let us call the horizon to which I just referred the *perceptual horizon.* (Or, less exactly, the *common sense horizon.*) This notion of horizon will be of special help later in understanding scientific knowing. In the meantime, however, we must turn our attention to the horizon defined not by our sense organs but by our power of understanding, the far wider horizon that is the *intelligible horizon.*

QUESTIONS FOR REVIEW AND DISCUSSION

1. Why is it hard (two reasons) to notice the structure of sense perception?

2. What are the main features of all the objects that you find yourself confronted with?

3. What is meant by the "subjective pole" of the act of perceiving?

4. What does it mean to say that sense perception is unavoidably "perspectival"?

8. Merleau-Ponty calls this a "point-horizon structure" in *Phenomenology of Perception,* 68, 102.

5. What is meant by the "inexhaustibility" of any perceived object?

6. What is remarkable about perceiving objects as still, unmoving?

7. What is meant here by the "world-giving" aspect of perception?

8. Which is correct: "The world is in me" or "I am in the world"?

9. Can you identify four senses in which perceiving is "inclusive"?

chapter 5

BEYOND PERCEIVING: SOME ASPECTS OF KNOWING

I walk to the window, gaze a moment at the lawn and the palm trees, but I also see a small brown object scurry across the lawn. A cat or a squirrel? My uncertainty vanishes almost instantly, since the creature goes straight up the trunk of a palm tree with a nimbleness beyond that of any cat. About the same time I also notice that the morning sun is pouring into the window and since it can fade things inside, I lower and adjust the venetian blind to block the light.

In these perfectly ordinary experiences we have a vignette of the interrelation between human sense perception and an activity that normally goes with it and beyond it, what I shall call *ordinary knowing* (in the stricter sense of the word, to distinguish it from the broader use of the word, which includes perception). Let us explore this.

5.1 UNCOVERING THE UNIVERSAL IN THE PARTICULAR

The above experiences of viewing a lawn, a tree, an animal, and sunlight in a room are *perceptual* experiences, and in particular, visual experiences. In that latter respect the example is unduly narrow, but given what was discussed in the previous chapter we may easily allow for the inclusion of other bodily senses as well. The example illustrates the *understanding* of a perceptual experience, grasping its intelligible meaning.

The first thing to notice is hard to notice: that I take for granted that what I am seeing is in fact a lawn and palm trees. After our earlier examination of the objectivity of sense perception I am satisfied that it is indeed external objects that I am viewing. What is of special interest here, however, is that without hesitation I *recognize* these things as palm trees and a lawn.

Being neither a biologist nor a botanist, I haven't the faintest idea of what may be the true essences of palm tree, lawn, and squirrel, but like you I have at least a kind of practical, working notion, based on experience, of what those particular things look like and act like. But in recognizing these things as lawn, palm trees, and squirrel I was grasping in them something that transcends them. I was looking at a very particular palm tree, at a particular time and place and with its particular shape and size, yet I grasped in it something that presumably belongs to all palm trees. (I say "presumably" in acknowledgment, as I have already confessed, that I really don't know its botanical nature. Yet I do, by and large, succeed in distinguishing palm trees from almost anything else.)

But herein lies a puzzle. "Palm tree" names a universal concept, a concept free of the particularities of space and time, of here and now. Yet the tree before me is altogether particular, of a very definite shape and most decidedly here and now. How is it, then, that this altogether particular and individual tree has given rise in my mind to a concept that is free of the limitations of space and time? And how do I successfully attribute the universal character "palm tree" to this here-now individual thing?[1]

---

1. This is really the problem of how any predication is possible at all. If I say, "My soup is hot," I am attributing a universal characteristic (hotness) to this particular bowl of soup. No one doubts that by and large we do this successfully, but *how* do we do it? What is happening here? This is an instance of the venerable philosophic "problem of the universals," much debated especially in the twelfth century. For a delightful and eye-opening glimpse into this debate and its significance, see Etienne Gilson, *The Unity of Philosophical Experience*, Part One.

Now it won't do to say, as some have, that this is merely a matter of classification for convenience's sake; that in saying (or thinking) "lawn," "palm tree," and "squirrel" I am not making any claim about what they "really are," but simply dealing with them in a pragmatic way by classifying and attaching certain names to them. But that way of brushing aside the problem won't do, because it amounts to the old and untenable position of "nominalism," which held that the only thing that specifically similar objects, such as two palm trees, actually have in common is the *name* that we attribute to them for purposes of convenience. But the reason our classification usually succeeds is that we only give the name "palm trees" to palm trees and not to oaks or geraniums. We have to recognize something intrinsic to palm trees not found in oaks or geraniums before we can give them the right names. Recognition must come before classification if it is going to work, and so the puzzle is still there.

Geometric examples help illuminate this puzzle. Suppose you consider the notion "triangle" (restricting ourselves to a Euclidean plane). To help you think of it and probe its intelligibility you find it helpful to draw, or at least to imagine, some particular triangle. Now of course nothing that you can draw with a pencil or with chalk is a real geometric triangle. For one thing, it is physically impossible to draw (or imagine) lines that are perfectly straight, still less to draw lines that have no thickness at all. Next, even if you *could* draw a geometric triangle, it would still be a particular kind of triangle and in a particular place. It is quite impossible to draw "triangle in general," yet that is what you are *thinking* when you assent to the proof that the sum of the interior angles of any plane triangle must be a straight angle. Similarly, when you grant the cogency of the Pythagorean theorem about right triangles you understand that the reasoning and the conclusion apply to any right triangle whatsoever, independently of the particularities of the triangle that happens to be drawn or imagined in the demonstration. Your mind thinks beyond what your eyes see, for your mind thinks "any old right triangle," not "this particular right triangle."

So whether you are confronting a particular palm tree and thinking "palm tree" (universal), or contemplating a particular drawn figure and thinking universal "triangle," your mind has somehow recognized, because it has disclosed, a characteristic of that particular tree or triangle that it shares with indefinitely many others. Call this disclosing activity of the mind its *illuminative function*. At this juncture I do not attempt to explain how my mind (or better, how I) do this. I just know that I do do it, and that in itself is remarkable.[2] In this illuminative or universalizing activity my mind is able to get beyond the limitations of space and time that are found in the biological activities of my sense organs and disclose universal intelligibilities that transcend the limitations of space and time.

Now it is one thing to reveal the universal character latent within a particular, and another to grasp the meaning or intelligibility of that character. There is an analogy to this distinction that goes clear back to Aristotle. Consider the necessity of light for sight. In total darkness you can't see an apple even if it is right in front of you. The apple *by itself* is not visible; it is only visible in the presence of light. When you shine a light on it, however, the act of lighting up the apple and thus making it actually visible is not the same act as your consequent seeing of the apple. The illuminating and the seeing are different *kinds* of activities, even though one is required for the other. Similarly, the activity that your mind somehow performs in getting at the universal character of the particular that is grasped by the senses, and the following act of *understanding,* of grasping the meaning of that character, are two interrelated but distinct activities. It is one thing to disclose the universal character "tree" within a particular tree, another to understand it so as to be able to distinguish it from other intelligibilities.

5.2   GRASPING THE MEANING OF UNIVERSAL CONCEPTS: UNDERSTANDING

Think back to elementary geometry and set aside the problem of *how* your mind is able to discover the universal concept "triangle."

2. In the Aristotelian-Thomistic tradition, this illuminative capacity of the mind was called the "agent" (or "activating") intellect.

What is happening when you ponder the notion "triangle"? When, for instance, you run through the proof that the sum of the interior angles of any (plane) triangle must be a straight angle, you *grasp something of the meaning of triangle*. Beginning with a drawn or imagined representation of triangle, not with a real (geometric) triangle, your mind has, by its illuminative activity, not only presented to you for contemplation the universal notion triangle, it then proceeds to explore the intelligibility of this notion, and it does this, typically, in such a series of theorems as one finds in Euclid. This activity of your mind—better, of you through your mind—that consists in grasping the intelligibility found in the universal concepts the mind discloses in your sensible experience, I shall call *ordinary understanding*. In it, for instance, I consider what it means to be a regular polygon, or what the derivative of a function means.

Notice at least two characteristics of such activity. First, it seems evidently *immaterial*. Of its very nature, in what it does, it transcends the limitations of space and time, and this is also true of its objects. That is clearly seen in mathematical examples which all have a universal character. It is also true of the universal concepts derived from sensible things. My senses grasp this tree as this-here-now-object, but my mind grasps it as an instance of "tree," a character or essence not confined to this particular tree.

No matter how this takes place—and it does take place—my activity of ordinary understanding is not a material activity and cannot be the activity of a purely material capacity, such as the external senses. I have been calling this capacity "mind," and I shall continue to do so without claiming to have established much more about it than that it is my inbuilt capacity to perform those acts of understanding that I do in fact perform. These acts are evidently immaterial, since they are not themselves limited by the conditions of space and time, and I therefore refer to them as "mental."

The activity of understanding is also an *immanent* activity, an activity taking place within me. It does not produce anything other than itself, and the activities we have so far considered have all been theoretic or contemplative rather than ordered to external activity.

Finally, I notice that understanding, of its nature, is *self-reflexive*. It is, as it were, diaphanous, wholly present to itself in its own acting, so that by it, I at the same time know and also know that I know. This seems to me an undeniable fact of experience—though it has indeed been denied. The reason that some thinkers have thought it paradoxical or even impossible lies in the natural tendency to assimilate understanding to a material or neurological activity of the senses or the brain. As we already noted, the eye cannot see its own seeing, for that would require a meta-eye to do the seeing of the seeing, and so on, *ad infinitum*. The material basis of seeing is at the root of this impossibility of complete self-presence. No extended body and no material activity can be wholly present to itself, but only one part present to another part. Furthermore the *object* of seeing, which is an illuminated colored body, is very different from the *act* of seeing.

That need not be the case, however, and indeed it is not the case, for the immaterial activity that is understanding. The object of that activity is a present, immaterial intelligibility (say, the form "triangle" or "tree"). Now according to what we saw in regard to perception, the perceiver and the perceived are united in a single activity. So in the act of understanding, the person understanding and the thing understood are united in the single activity that is understanding. But that activity, since it is immaterial, has no parts to keep it apart from itself. Also, it is wholly characterized by the intelligible form that is its object. As an analogy, consider the light of a slide projector after it has passed through the slide and is on its way to the screen. It carries in itself the pattern of the slide. In somewhat the same way, understanding "tree" or "triangle" means that the activity of understanding is itself characterized by the form or pattern "tree" or "triangle" that was received from the material object.

In the chapter on perception we saw that when you perceive a tree, you in a certain sense (that is, in the intentional order) *become* that tree. You don't, of course, physically turn into the tree but you perceptually *act* "this tree" in perceiving it. Similarly, in *understanding* "tree" or "triangle" your act of understanding is itself patterned by the form tree or triangle.

Now this immaterial activity patterned by an immaterial form ("tree" or "triangle") *is itself intelligible.* And since, lacking parts, it is wholly present to itself, there is no reason why it should not automatically *understand itself* in its understanding. That is, by the very nature of the immaterial act of understanding, *you can't help understanding yourself as understanding* when you understand—and that is just your experience of *self-awareness.* In understanding anything, you at the same time understand that you do understand it, and there is really nothing paradoxical about that. Indeed it could not be otherwise, given the immaterial nature of the act and its object.

So far, then, our analysis of those most ordinary experiences at the window has led us to distinguish two different acts of the mind: (1) an activity by which the mind discloses to itself universal forms somehow latent within particular objects, and (2) understanding, which is the activity of grasping the meaning of those intelligible forms. This does not yet explain what happened with regard to the squirrel. Something else is going on here.

5.3   AFFIRMING EXTRAMENTAL EXISTENCE

My momentary perplexity about the squirrel, and my resolution of it, reveals still another facet of mental experience. In the instant of first seeing the squirrel I was not yet sure whether it was a squirrel or a cat; both ideas sprang to mind. Size, configuration, and behavior quickly resolved the uncertainty, but the fact remains that not one but two different notions competed for a moment in my mind, and I was not instantly ready to decide between the two. From this alone I realize that it is one thing to *entertain* a universal idea, another to attribute it to or *affirm* it of a perceived object. To "think squirrel" is not the same as to say to myself "That's a squirrel." This is clear also from my capacity to think of winged horses or of unicorns. I can think them without supposing that they actually exist outside my mind.

In looking out the window, then, I was not only stimulated to *understand* the abstract notions "lawn" and "palm tree," I also implicitly and immediately was affirming to myself "that's a lawn and those are palm trees." And regarding the animal, I quickly affirmed "that's a squirrel (rather than a cat)."

We have, then, three distinct activities of the mind involved in the experience at the window. First there is an illuminative activity, disclosing universal characters. This is immediately followed by understanding, which grasps the meaning of those characters. These first two activities are so intimately united—the first making the second possible—that we may for our purposes treat them as two aspects of a single activity. The third activity is that of affirming the extramental existence of something that has those understood characters. This affirmation has traditionally been called *judgment*.

Because understanding an intelligible form and affirming that it is actually found in something outside the mind are two different activities, there is room for error in passing from understanding to affirmation. The contemplation in understanding of an intelligible form, such as "triangle" or "tree," can hardly be called either true or false. "Triangle" and "tree," merely as understood concepts, are neither true nor false. Truth or falsity, in the usual sense, belong to affirmation or judgment, not to pure understanding, and the truth of affirmation depends on the evidence on the basis of which one moves from understanding to affirmation. In mathematics and logic the evidence is found in the internal consistency of the concepts themselves, but in affirmations about matters of fact the evidence can be complicated and even inconclusive. In the case of the squirrel, the evidence lay in what the animal looked like, when observed more closely, and in how it acted. The process, however, by which we are often forced to reach affirmations can, unlike that for the case of my recognizing the squirrel, be long and tortuous and thus easily subject to error. Things are even more complicated when it comes to physical science, as we shall soon see.

Granted, then, that there is the possibility of error in forming our affirmations about the character of extramental existents, what seems to be the internal structure of the act of affirmation? We can approximate it by putting together what we noted in the second chapter about "fundamental" perception, the experience of being acted upon, and so forth, and what we just saw in the previous section about the self-reflexivity of knowing.

That is, we affirm, because the fact is immediately present to us, that we are in the experiential presence of an extramental object that, for plausible reasons, seems to embody the intelligible forms we are entertaining. Even if we haven't the least idea just *what* we are encountering, we still feel ourselves experiencing or confronted by an object, so that the most primitive form of existential judgment is simply "Something (experienced) *is.*" More often, we find that we are entertaining certain intelligible forms as characterizing that object which is influencing us. "There is a squirrel," for instance. There is no doubting our experience, both of being acted upon and of entertaining such forms. The catch lies in whether these forms really characterize the encountered object. It is evident, then, that there is room, indeed a need, for a whole theory of what constitutes adequate evidence for such affirmations.[3] What can, at least, be said here is this: my affirmation (say, that that is a squirrel) embodies the self-reflexive assent to the given presence to me, within the act of perceiving, of an active (on me) bodily being that gives evidence of having that certain form of being and acting that I identify as belonging to a squirrel.

It is worth noting here that our knowing is not confined to material conditions. There lies open at least the possibility of recognizing the value of immaterial entities, such as friendship, or the existence of immaterial beings, should there be any, such as God.

The perceptive reader may have noticed that under this heading of "affirming extramental existence" I have not yet mentioned

---

3. The classic, one could well say monumental, contemporary study of the acts of the mind and of the process of arriving at affirmations through evidence is that of Bernard F. Lonergan, S.J., *Insight: A Study in Human Understanding.* A more traditional Thomistic treatment may be found in R. J. Henle, S.J., *Theory of Knowledge.*

that type of extramental existence that is paramount, the most fundamental of all. It is the affirmation of living and communicating with other human beings. The human being is not a solitary "I"-entity but a "we"-entity. Our active interrelationship with others is the most fundamental experience we have, hence is the proper beginning of any philosophical reflection.[4] Yet, under the technical name of the problem of "intersubjectivity" it became for some philosophers one of the most intractable philosophical puzzles of the twentieth century.[5]

It is easy to see how this would be a problem for anyone holding anything like a representational epistemology. John Locke, for instance. Suppose you are a friend of Locke's and go to visit him. What, according to his own philosophy, happens when he recognizes you walking into the room? He is suddenly confronted with some new visual sense data (he just calls them "ideas"): certain colored shapes, accompanied by certain sounds (which he interprets as footsteps), by a feeling of pressure in his right hand during the handshake, and perhaps by a smell that he associates with your kind of aftershave. From these colored shapes, and these sensations of sounds, tactile feelings, and smell, he must *infer* to your body that is beyond his direct experience and that is not really colored or noisy or smelly, at least not the way his sensations are. But even if the inference is valid, Locke has still not gotten to *you* but only to your body. From the apparent behavior of your body he will than have to make a further inference to your mind.

But is such an account believable? Do we experience other persons in this piecemeal fashion? It is reported that when the problem of how we know minds other than our own was mentioned to

4. This fundamentally social nature of the human person is developed by W. Norris Clarke in "The 'We Are' of Interpersonal Dialogue as the Starting Point of Metaphysics," ch. 2 of his *Explorations in Metaphysics;* see also his *Person and Being.*

5. Thus, Edmund Husserl begins the fifth of his *Cartesian Meditations* with an "Exposition of the problem of experiencing someone else." In my own opinion he does not succeed in solving this "problem," a problem that does not come naturally to anyone but arose for Husserl because of the particular assumptions he made about philosophical method.

Whitehead he exclaimed: "Hang it all! *Here we are.* We don't go behind that, we begin with it."[6]

5.4   SOME OTHER ASPECTS OF KNOWING: VALUES AND PRACTICAL KNOWING

Two other aspects of ordinary knowing need to be at least briefly mentioned at this point. The first is its *value dimension.* In the chapters on perception we noted the existence of the immediate feeling of value or importance that forms part of the very activity that is sense perceiving (in what I called "fundamental perceiving"). This value that is *felt* in perception is at the same time consciously recognized within the self-reflexive activity that is ordinary knowing. We not only *feel* influenced by an object, we know that we are so influenced. But since knowing is immaterial, it has the capacity to embrace a wider spectrum of value than does fundamental perception. For to feel influenced by another body, or even to feel the importance of color vision, is a purely perceptual activity. But to feel the value of friendship or of a work of art is another activity, beyond sense perception. Here we have merely a more explicit spelling out of Whitehead's insight, quoted in the last chapter, that our enjoyment of actuality is in fact a value experience, a realization of worth, good or bad.

This sensitivity to value in our ordinary knowing lies at the heart, in fact, of all our specifically human actions. For in all our deliberate actions we *aim at some good.* Having grasped the value of some possibility for action, we may then strive for it in our actions. We go to the movies or a ball game for the sake of enjoyment. We go to college and select a major in order to gain enrichment of mind, not only for its own sake but for the sake of making a living and of making a difference to the world we live in. Without the aim at recognized value we would do nothing at all; we would be as good as dead.

This brings out another essential factor in ordinary knowing: namely, that it is open to the *possible* as well as to the actual. And

6. Quoted by William Ernest Hocking in "Whitehead as I Knew Him," 8.

this, in fact, marks another puzzle. It is remarkable enough that the mind is able to extract from a particular, material object its own character of universal intelligibility. But how does it occur to the mind to entertain other such characters, not yet realized but *relevant* to the present situation and potentially realizable from it? It is precisely such relevant but as yet unrealized possibilities for value realization that constitute our *aim* or goal in whatever we do. Since such possibilities are not presently realized they cannot be material, yet they are in fact recognized by the mind and serve as the lure for all our deliberate activities.

These considerations about aims or goals as originative of our deliberate activities bring naturally to light the second function of mental activities that I want to mention in this section: *practical knowing*. We have mainly been concerned with the theoretic or speculative aspect of knowing, by which we grasp meanings. In practical knowing we utilize this understanding toward the pursuit of our aims. Thus, practical knowing is intimately related to the recognition of values as aims.

We saw this already, in fact, in the simple events that I described at the window. I not only recognized lawn, trees, and a squirrel, I also realized a practical need, namely to keep direct sunlight from fading things in the room. I also recognized that closing the venetian blind would do the trick. That was an instance of practical knowing, the recognition of suitable means to a desired end, and there followed the willing and carrying out of that simple activity.

Though we have no room in this slender book to devote more space to practical knowing, it is clearly of paramount importance in human activities, whether of us as individuals or as bonded in society.

5.5 PERCEIVING, KNOWING, AND HORIZONS

We may now note, as a kind of summary, some ways in which ordinary knowing goes beyond sense perceiving. The main way is that it gives to perceiving its *self-reflexivity,* so that human perceiving is always conscious perceiving. We perceive with our senses, but at the same time we realize (even if subconsciously) that we do this. In the above reflections we have explained something of the metaphysical structure of this self-reflexivity inasmuch as we have pointed to the self-presence of an immaterial act that is itself an object of understanding.

This self-consciousness extends also to our sensory feeling of being influenced by other things in the world. In other words, it enables us to make that sensory feeling intelligible. It further extends to our feeling of the inherent value in our sense perceptions, but it goes beyond that inasmuch as it extends also to the consciousness of immaterial values, such as that of friendship.

Recalling the notion of *horizon* from the previous chapter, we may now ask what horizon of reality is open to us in ordinary knowing. That horizon, of course, is where we find all the sorts of things that ordinary knowing has as its possible objects. The horizon just *is*, if you like, the set of all possible objects that ordinary knowing can recognize.

With ordinary knowing we are far beyond the horizon of sense perception (what I have called the perceptual horizon), which is bounded by the sensible objects. What we can *think* far outstrips what we can see, hear, or touch. Indeed, we have seen that knowing must be an immaterial activity whose objects are themselves immaterial. True, in some sense we know material things but we know them just because we grasp in them their intelligible natures realized within the confines of their bodies.

Another way of illustrating this point is to ask ourselves what are all the sorts of things we would like to know. The astronomer studies the heavens not particularly because he or she expects to gain any practical advantage out of such knowledge but mainly for the sheer satisfaction of *knowing* what is happening in the heavens and what has been the history of the universe. And theologians try to open their minds to understand, in some limited way, a Being that is altogether immaterial.

That the horizon of knowing reaches that far is a clear indication that our natural way of knowing, which is to recognize the intelligibility of the material objects of our sense experience, is limited not by our minds themselves but by the limitation of where our minds naturally have to look in order to find something to understand. That is, our natural human way of understanding begins in reflection on what we sense. If there are any Pure Intelligences, which, like Aristotle's First Mover, understand simply by understanding themselves, we are not they, even though Descartes gave that a try. Our drive to know does not stop with the material objects of our sense experience but it necessarily starts there.

We conclude, then, that the horizon of our ordinary knowing is complex: it seems in itself limitless, though it must start with, and consequently largely be constrained by, the limitations of our sense powers. Scientific knowing, to which we shall now turn our attention, manages to enlarge this sensible base of knowing. Science and, in their own ways, literature, philosophy, and theology, are ways of liberating our minds from their natural confinement to our physical senses.[7] When William Blake spoke of seeing a world in a grain of sand he was referring not to sense perception but to knowing.

QUESTIONS FOR REVIEW AND DISCUSSION

1. Why is there a puzzle about recognizing a palm tree as a palm tree?

2. What is the nature of a universal idea?

3. Why is it not good enough to say that we simply *impose* universal ideas onto particular objects for purposes of classification, and that's all the existence they have in the particulars?

4. How do you know that, in recognizing a palm tree as a palm tree, the mind has performed what might be called an "illuminative" function?

---

7. The reader will find a more developed and more technical account of the relation between knowing and sensing in Edward Pols, *Radical Realism: Direct Knowing in Science and Philosophy*. Though his approach is rather different from the one used above, his conclusions are much the same.

5. Show why this illuminative function cannot be identical to the activity of *understanding* the meaning of the resulting universal idea.

6. Roughly, what happens in *understanding*?

7. How do you know that the activity of understanding is, in itself, immaterial?

8. What is meant here by calling that activity "mental"?

9. What is meant here by "judgment" and how does it differ from understanding?

10. What are the three distinct activities of the mind that are involved in concluding, "I'm seeing a squirrel"?

11. What is a principal source of error in such a judgment?

12. Why is human knowing at least open to the possibility of recognizing the existence of immaterial beings?

13. What is meant by the "value dimension" of knowing?

14. How does friendship, or art, illustrate the immateriality of the mind?

15. What does the possible have to do with acting for an aim?

16. In just what sense can we say we *know* material things?

17. What is the main limitation naturally inherent in human knowing? Is it a limitation of our minds?

chapter 6

SCIENTIFIC KNOWING AND THE WORLD OF SCIENCE

In a passage that has become famous, Sir Arthur Eddington posed a dilemma about the relation between what our senses tell us and what science tells us. He wrote, in part:

> I have settled down to the task of writing these lectures and have drawn up my chairs to my two tables. Two tables! Yes, there are duplicates of every object about me—two tables, two chairs, two pens. . . .
>
> . . . One of them has been familiar to me from earliest years. It is a commonplace object of that environment which I call the world. How shall I describe it? It has extension; it is comparatively permanent; it is coloured; above all it is *substantial.* . . .
>
> Table No. 2 is my scientific table. It is a more recent acquaintance and I do not feel so familiar with it. It does not belong to the world previously mentioned—that world which spontaneously appears around me when I open my eyes. . . . It is part of a world which in more devious ways has forced itself on my attention. My scientific table is mostly emptiness. Sparsely scattered in that emptiness are numerous electric charges rushing about with great speed. . . .

There is nothing *substantial* about my second table. It is nearly all empty space—space pervaded, it is true, by fields of force, but these are assigned to the category of "influences," not of "things.". . .

I need not tell you that modern physics has by delicate test and remorseless logic assured me that my second scientific table is the only one which is really there.[1]

Which avenue of knowledge are we to believe—the testimony of our senses, or the scientific description of an eerie world unlike anything we can directly experience? Do we have to agree that the scientific table is the only table that really exists, so that the sensible table is only a kind of natural illusion? This perplexity about the relation between the common sense world and the scientific world forces us to examine the unusual way of knowing that is scientific knowing. We do this best, I think, by re-examining and enlarging the concept of *horizon* that has already been introduced.[2]

6.1   MORE ABOUT HORIZONS: A MATTER OF MEANING

We already noted the delimiting aspect of a horizon—as, for instance, that the visual horizon is limited to the natural capacities of our external senses, so that we can't directly sense anything outside that range. But there is also a positive correlation between our capacity to sense or know and the objects that that capacity picks out.

This point is obvious enough with regard to sense perception. Just as the kind of film we put into a camera determines the sort of pictures it can take, so our ability—or lack of it—to see certain colors defines what sorts of objects we can perceive.

---

1. Arthur Eddington, *The Nature of the Physical World,* xi–xiv; emphasis in the original.

2. The following development of ideas is adapted from the illuminating but technical essay, "Horizon, Objectivity and Reality in the Physical Sciences" by Patrick A. Heelan, S.J. I attempt here to simplify and adapt Heelan's ideas for the more limited purposes of this essay.

There is another important, positive relation between what we contribute to sensation and what we find in it. This consists in the *interpretative anticipations* that we bring *to* our sense experience, and which, in turn, determine the *meaning* for us of what we find. The world we find is pretty much the world we were prepared to find, the world we were looking for.

Here is an illustration of what I mean. Suppose there are three persons, an Army general, an artist, and a real estate developer, standing side by side and looking out over a valley. The general sees the valley as an avenue of attack for himself or for the enemy. The artist sees the valley as an interrelation of hues and shapes suggestive of a creative reintegration in a painting. The real estate developer sees the valley as a potential source of development and profit.

Although all three are *looking at* the same valley, there is a clear sense in which each *sees* a different valley. Let me be clear about what I am claiming. I am not saying that although each sees the same valley, each *interprets* what he or she sees in a different way. There would be nothing paradoxical about that. No, I mean that although they are looking at the same valley, what each *sees* is a *different* valley from what the other two see. For what each one sees is in fact already a function of the structured set of anticipations that he or she brings to the experience.

As was pointed out in Chapter 2, *there is no world-in-itself that we attain in sense perception* but always a world already involved in our act of perceiving it (thus a relational world), and consequently a world already attuned to our powers of perceiving. That is what relational realism means. For instance, the color of light falling upon an automobile determines the color of the car we see. We do not perceive the car in itself but the *appearing* car, and the appearing car is already conditioned by the available light. In a similar way, the three persons looking at a valley *do not see the valley in itself but an appearing valley*. By "appearing" we now include its interpretative, psychological, or intellectual "appearance," *the valley in its dimension of meaning*. The valley that each one sees, the appearing or experienced valley, is already conditioned not only in its visual aspect, as by the available light, but in its dimension of meaning that flows from the observer's interests and anticipations. The valley that each person *sees* is not the physical valley in itself but an *experiential* valley, a relational valley, that is already a function of the structured anticipations that each brings to the experiencing. Thus the appearing valley for each is not just a visible valley but a meaningful valley, and in that sense each sees a different valley from what the others see.

In his seminal book, *The Structure of Scientific Revolutions,* the late Thomas S. Kuhn affirms a similar position though he freely grants that he is unable to explain just how this is possible. He writes: "In a sense that I am unable to explicate further, the proponents of competing paradigms [such as the Aristotelian and the Newtonian] practice their trades *in different worlds*" (my emphasis).[3] The epistemological viewpoint I have adopted in this essay, however, especially about the relationality of perception and about horizons, does explicate how different people, and especially different sorts of methodic inquirers, experientially *see different worlds.* What they see is very much a matter of their frames of mind, that is, of the structure of their questioning attitude toward the world and of their anticipations as to what they may find. And such anticipations are indeed structured, for they map the data of the senses against a whole network of interrelated interests and expectations, and those interests are in turn a function of the person's aims.

6.2   DISCOVERY STRUCTURES AND WORLDS

I call such a structured anticipation a *discovery structure,* and in terms of discovery structures we shall be able to make sense of the worlds of common sense and of science as distinct ways of human knowing. A discovery structure stands in a *polar relation* to the world that it reveals, for the structure's function is precisely to reveal a certain sort of world. So when we investigate the nature of scientific knowing we are inquiring into the discovery structure

---

3.   Thomas S. Kuhn, *The Structure of Scientific Revolutions,* 150.

peculiar to science and also into the scientific world, or scientific horizon, that is disclosed by that structure. What then are the elements of the discovery structure of science, and what is the character of its world?

There are of course many forms of science, and we can't consider them all. But there is no need to do that anyway, since, as we shall see, all or most of them seem to share a distinctive discovery structure, one that involves the use of *instruments*. And since physics is in some sense the simplest of these sciences, not being involved, for instance, with biological or psychological processes, I shall use physics as a paradigm, and leave applications to other particular sciences to the interest of the reader. Also, this sketch of the discovery structure and of the world of science will be carried out on a very elementary level, but that should suffice for the purposes of our inquiry.

6.3   THE HORIZON OF PHYSICAL SCIENCE

What one immediately notices about the discovery structure of science, as compared with our everyday anticipations and concerns about the world, is science's deliberate narrowness of interest. The physicist is concerned with just those aspects of experience—or rather, of instrumental experience—that can be interpreted in terms of such characteristics as position, momentum, mass, electric charge, and so forth. The physicist, acting precisely as a physicist, is not concerned with human values such as friendship, nor with interpersonal relationships, nor with ethics or aesthetics. This is not a criticism of physics or of any other science, only a recognition that an important reason for science's success is that it has narrowed its range of interest very sharply and so left out of consideration all sorts of other issues that would stand in the way of scientific accuracy and progress.

Correspondingly—by the polarity between discovery structures and the horizons they establish—the world as described by science must lack just those aspects that are omitted in science's discovery structure. This is not a flaw in the world described by science, it is just a natural limitation of it. The mistake would be to confuse the scientific world with all other possible or actual worlds, to suppose that the scientific world is the only world.

Let me make this clearer. A discovery structure defines a *horizon* of all the possible objects recognizable by that structure, and the sum of all such objects may be called the particular *world* corresponding to that discovery structure. Now, as there can be indefinitely many discovery structures, and consequently indefinitely many corresponding horizons and worlds of objects filling up those horizons, so we may define *World* (with a capital *W*) as the totality of objects attainable by all possible discovery structures. The World may be said to correspond to the horizon of all possible horizons. But there is no horizon of all possible horizons that is attainable by us humans. That would indeed be a God's-eye view, but one that we have no access to.

So each world—or perhaps we could say each level or sort of reality available to us—is defined by the discovery structure giving rise to it, but none is definitive in the sense of being the all-comprehensive World. And the scientific world bears just those limitations that are defined by its deliberately narrow scientific discovery structure.

Another notable feature of the scientific discovery structure, especially that of physics, is its almost exclusive involvement with mathematics. That the world is an embodied mathematics is an idea that dates back not only to Galileo but even to Pythagoras (sixth century B.C.), and it lies at the heart of modern fundamental physical theory. The models in terms of which physics understands experimental evidence are basically mathematical, not imaginative miniaturizations of the macroscopic objects of human experience. Such mathematical models, as forming an essential part of the discovery structure of contemporary physics, yield a scientific world that is essentially mathematical. Such a procedure gives a penetrating insight into the world discoverable by scientific instruments— but exactly into *that* world, not into every world.

I have twice mentioned instruments, but only in passing. It is time to give explicit attention to their role in scientific knowing, for as we shall see, instruments make practically all the difference.

An instrument is a kind of vicarious observer—a substitute perceiver—that we employ to tell us something that we would not otherwise perceive (or at least not do it conveniently). It is a go-between that relates us to the world. The fuel gauge on your car is an example of a very simple instrument. It tells you something about the gasoline in your tank that you could hardly know in any other convenient way. By familiarity we commonly bypass in our minds the intermediate status of an instrument and read its significance directly. Thus we identify the position of the needle with the gas in the tank; our experience is of seeing a full tank rather than of seeing where a needle stands.

Though the fuel gauge is indeed an instrument, it does not function in the technical way critical to distinguishing scientific knowing from ordinary perception, since the gasoline in the tank is in various ways directly observable by ordinary perception. But let us shift the example. Suppose there has been a lightning storm and you have reason to wonder whether a certain radio station has escaped damage to its antennas and is still broadcasting. So you turn on your radio and set it to the station's frequency. When you hear a program emanating from that frequency you know that the station is still broadcasting.

Notice that although the radio is an object belonging to the everyday (perceptual) world, you are now *using* it as an instrument to tell you something about another world whose horizon does not fall within the perceptual horizon. You can't directly sense radio waves, but you can affirm their existence because you recognize that they are "perceived" by the radio you are using as an instrument. In this example the instrumentality of the radio lies precisely in the *use* that is made of it, even though it normally functions only in the perceptual world.

I propose, following Heelan (see note 2 of this chapter), that what is most distinctive of the discovery structure of physics, and consequently of its horizon, is that it invokes the use of instruments for attaining its objects. It is the instrument that "experiences" the magnetic field or the path of a subatomic particle, not direct human perception. The physicist directly observes the reaction of the instrument to its "experience," and physical theory enables the physicist to interpret that reaction in terms of events or objects that the physicist cannot directly experience.

Thus what a scientific experiment *attains* as its object (the magnetic field or the subatomic particle) is never part of the perceptual world of direct experience. Thus the discovery structure of science *sets up a different horizon of knowing* from that of direct sensory experience.

This view, if it is correct, discredits the common conception that scientific instruments simply enhance or refine sense perception rather than establish a different kind of knowing altogether. Many of us wear corrective lenses to improve our vision; we have all used magnifying glasses to help us read tiny details; the laboratory technician routinely uses an optical microscope to do the same thing with much greater precision. Then there is the electron microscope with which even single atoms have been observed.

Now it seems undeniable that eyeglasses enhance ordinary perception rather than constitute what I have described above as the instruments peculiar to scientific knowing. The same can be said of magnifying glasses and optical microscopes. They extend the range of sense perception but they do not act as vicarious observers. The electron microscope, however, is designed, on the basis of theory, to paint us a sensible picture constructed from its own, insensible interaction with reality on an atomic level. That interaction is an activity that radically differs from our own sensation, and hence constitutes a different horizon of knowing. The horizon of ordinary perception and the horizon of scientific knowing are quite literally *incommensurable*.

Notice how this view agrees with what was established in an earlier chapter concerning *relational realism*. By that theory, you the knower are united with the object of knowing precisely in and by your activity of knowing, an activity that is the actuality of both you the knower and of the known all at once. The object presents itself to you only through its activity on you, and in the case of scientific objects that activity is always mediated by the use of an instrument. (You can already begin to see the solution of Eddington's paradox.)

6.4   THE SCIENTIFIC WORLD AND THE PERCEPTUAL WORLD

Is then the world described by science the real world? The question, I am afraid, is badly put even though it seems very natural. For it seems to suppose that there is just one real world that we can talk about and that is somehow independent of the discovery structures that define it and enable us to attain it and thus affirm its reality.

What, after all, enables us to affirm the real existence of anything? Recall what was said in section 5.3, p. 69, about affirming the existence of something in the perceptual world:

> my affirmation (say, that that is a squirrel) embodies the self-reflexive assent to the given presence to me, within the act of perceiving, of an active (on me) bodily being that gives evidence of having that certain form of being and acting that I identify as belonging to a squirrel.

How might such an affirmation of existence in the perceptual world be adapted to affirming existence in the scientific world? Let us try something like this:

> My affirmation that certain electromagnetic (radio) waves exist (hence that a particular radio station is in fact broadcasting) embodies the self-reflexive assent to the given presence to me, within the act of perceiving, of an active (on me) physical instrument that gives evidence (here by its sound) of an interaction between it and the scientific entity in question (the radio waves).

The link between the behavior of the instrument and the radio waves is of course supplied by the underlying scientific theory (in this case, of electromagnetism) that forms part of the discovery structure of contemporary physics. That theory predicts that under certain circumstances a certain type of instrument should react in a certain sensibly perceivable way, given the nature of the mathematical model of electromagnetic waves. When, through the use of the instrument, I am aware that just such a reaction is occurring, I am justified in affirming the existence of those waves even though they belong to the scientific horizon that I can't directly experience. Notice, however, that my judgment that such waves "exist" is entirely a function of the theory I have brought to bear in order to understand the behavior of the instrument. For a different theory, those "waves" might have no meaning and would be replaced by some other model of reality. Once again, the "world" we deal with is perspectival to the intelligible structures that we bring to it.

This simple example fits the basic structure of the instrumental knowing processes of even the far more sophisticated techniques of contemporary physics. When the physicist employs detectors such as photographic film or cloud chambers to analyze high energy atomic processes, the tell-tale tracks are an instrumental sign of the presence of atomic or subatomic particles having particular characteristics of energy and charge. The direct interaction, of course, is between the particles and the detector, but the sensibly perceivable behavior of the detector grounds the affirmation of the existence, in the scientific world, of the particles.

How does this conclusion shed light on Eddington's paradox of the "two tables"? Is it true, as he says, that science has assured us that the scientific table is the only table that is real?

Science may say so, but only from its own point of view—from the limits of its own discovery structure. From that perspective, then, of course the table is made up of atoms that are not sensibly perceivable, that do not form a tactile continuity, and so forth. Science, however, cannot assure us that there is no other way of inquiring into reality, no other legitimate discovery structure, and no other world. Indeed, science itself cannot do without the structure of ordinary perception in the reading of its own instruments. Sooner or later in the instrumental process of measurement a scientist has to observe the digital readout of an instrument or the position of a needle or the curvature of a track. The scientist, then, relies on the everyday perceptual horizon as much as anyone else, but uses the perception of instruments to reveal the otherwise hidden

secrets of a world discernible only by means of the vicarious observation of instruments and the discovery structures (theories) that
give meaning to the record of that observation.

Hence Eddington was mistaken in supposing that only the
"scientific table" is real. The sensible object that we call a table is
surely real within the perceptual world, and sense experience is
itself indispensable to attaining the scientific world. In what sense
is the table also real in the scientific world? In this sense: that if you
subject parts of the table to a scientific analysis by means of various
sophisticated instruments you will conclude, by means of your
scientific theory, that it does indeed have an atomic structure.

Even so, would it be right to say that there are *two* tables, an
everyday table and a scientific table? What on earth would a scientific table be? "Table" is a concept that belongs to the everyday
horizon and so there is no place for "table" in the horizon defined
by science. Would it not then be more accurate to say that there is
just one *table*, and that it belongs to the everyday, perceptual world,
but that it is also capable of being subjected to an analysis by scientific instruments that reveal its inner structure in terms of the
discovery structures of contemporary scientific theory? It is wrong
to say that the table is not "really" smooth or brown or hard, for
that is just as we find it perceptibly. Those characteristics belong to
the everyday horizon, and the table has all of them. But it should
not seem paradoxical that if you subject the table to an analysis by
instruments suited to reveal the presence, in the scientific world, of
sensibly unperceivable entities, the instrumental reactions should
enable you to affirm a scientific atomic structure disclosed within
the everyday object that is a table.

We conclude then that the discovery structure of ordinary
sense perception, by which we perceive a sensible world, and that
of science, by which through instruments and theory we indi-
rectly come to know a world that lies beneath our senses, are
fundamentally different perspectives on reality and constitute fundamentally different horizons of reality. The objects filling those
respective horizons make up the everyday perceptual world on the

one hand and the scientific world on the other. Both worlds are real but real in different senses, inasmuch as they are functions of different sorts of activities constituted by different discovery structures logically different from each other.

The horizon of sense perception, and the horizon of scientific knowing by means of the vicarious experience of instruments, do not contradict but rather *complement* each other. Each tells us an authentic story, but the "world" described by the one is not the same as that described by the other, and we immediately entangle ourselves in paradoxes, such as that of Eddington, when we muddle these two horizons together. The scientific atom is real, but not real in the same sense as a pebble, for the atom belongs to the scientific horizon of knowing and the pebble belongs to the perceptual horizon.

Such a conclusion not only clarifies what is going on in science, it also suggests that still other horizons of knowing are possible as well, each one of which tells us something of its own about the World. One readily thinks, for instance, of a possible theological horizon, but in this short essay I do not propose to explore that possibility. I turn rather to that activity that is philosophy (in the traditional sense) in order to understand just what sort of activity it is, and whether it deserves the name of knowledge.

QUESTIONS FOR REVIEW AND DISCUSSION

1. What does it mean to say that the world we encounter is the world we were looking for?

2. Do three different people see three different valleys?

3. What is meant here by a "discovery structure"?

4. What are the advantages and the disadvantages of science's limitation of its interests?

5. What is the main general character of the *models* constructed by physics?

6. What is the function of an *instrument,* especially a scientific instrument? Why isn't the fuel gauge on your car a genuine scientific instrument? Is an ordinary radio a scientific instrument? Are eyeglasses?

7. What is wrong with asking which is the real table: the common sense table or the scientific table? How do you deal with Eddington's conclusion that the scientific table is the only table that is real?

chapter 7

PHILOSOPHIC KNOWING, PART I: SOME CLASSIC CASES

What is philosophy anyway, and is it a kind of knowing? Neither question deserves an offhand answer or one drawn out of the blue. Obviously the second question can't be answered before answering the first, and if you took a poll today you would probably find almost as many different notions of philosophy as philosophers you ask. So it is impossible to answer either question, let alone both, in a way that everyone would agree with. I shall, then, focus on just one of the competing respectable views, the view that seems persuasive to me as describing the most important sense of "philosophy" and its manner of knowing.

So as not to settle upon this sense of philosophy in an a priori fashion, I shall point to some outstanding historical precedents as exemplifying philosophy in its best sense. I have therefore selected four philosophers who span almost twenty-five hundred years, yet who share a fundamental conviction as to what they are doing as philosophers. The first two, from the classical flowering of philosophy in Greece, are virtually the founders of Western philosophy: Plato (427?–347 B.C.) and Aristotle. Unquestionably they represent philosophy in the traditional sense that I am accepting here. To them I add Saint Thomas Aquinas, who, besides being a theologian, arguably made the most penetrating philosophic advances of the high middle ages. To them I add, finally, Alfred North Whitehead, whom I consider to be the most significant metaphysician of the twentieth century.

But a difficulty presents itself. It would seem an impossible project to describe here, even in barest outline, the philosophical positions of four philosophic geniuses. Yet it isn't necessary to do that. The French philosopher Henri Bergson (1859-1941) has pointed out that there are two aspects to a person's philosophy. One is what you might call the "soul" of the philosophy, that central insight that colors and informs all the rest. He calls it a "single point" and goes on to say: "In this point is something simple, so extraordinarily simple that the philosopher has never succeeded in saying it. And that is why he went on talking all his life."[1]

The other aspect is the whole system of interrelated concepts that the philosopher devises in order to try to express the central insight in a way that can be communicated to others. It is this conceptual structure, with all its complications, that gets identified in people's minds with the system itself, although you would not understand the philosopher even if you memorized the whole conceptual structure but failed to grasp its central insight.

Now Bergson himself grants that one can at least approximate the central insight, especially if it is done by way of images or symbols. So that is what I shall endeavor to do in describing the philosophic positions of the above philosophers. I shall merely point to what I take to be their central insights from which everything else follows in their thinking.

7.1 FOUR CLASSIC CASES OF METAPHYSICS

7.1.1 Plato

Plato's philosophic view is best seen against the background of the earlier Greek philosophers. They were all preoccupied with *nature*

---

1. Henri Bergson, *The Creative Mind*, 108-9.

as they experienced it, a nature in constant change or flux, yet somehow also exhibiting regularity and stability. And they wanted to know more than just matters of fact—such as that a triangle with sides of 3, 4, and 5 units is a right triangle. The Egyptians already knew that, but it was the Greeks, notably Pythagoras, who wanted to know *why* that is so and why it could not be otherwise. For the first time, mathematical thinkers were not only aware of a mathematical fact, they understood it. So too they tried to understand why the seasons change and why acorns grow into oaks. They wanted to understand the changes taking place in nature.

It was Plato's intuition that the change we experience with our senses can be fully understood only in terms of something that does not change, something that is therefore impervious to the gnawing tooth of time. One of his most striking examples is that of beauty. It was Plato's insight that every changing, beautiful thing— say, a sunset, a rose, a human body, a personality—is beautiful just insofar as it shares or participates in the timeless pattern that is Beauty itself. If we sometimes get psychologically bowled over by particular beautiful things (whose beauty, after all, is limited and temporary, like that of the rose or the human body), what would it be like if we were somehow confronted with Beauty Itself, limitless and unfading?

So, thought Plato, the basic nature and the flowing characters of everything we experience with our bodily senses are intelligible only as constantly sharing in patterns of existence (his "Forms") that are timeless and unchanging. And since these Forms of existence are timeless and therefore indestructible, they are more fully real than material, perishable things that have only a shadowy kind of reality. And the timeless Forms likewise share in The Good, so that all reality has value just insofar as it is real.

Plato thus has a unified view of all reality in terms of a hierarchy of shared goodness and intelligibility. And the human person stands somehow in between—in between what is less real (material, bodily existence) and what is most real (the immaterial). We are called by nature to move away from the material and with our minds to press toward the immaterial, ultimately toward The Good itself. That is just what it means to be most fully human, and that is identical with the lifelong pursuit of the philosopher.

7.1.2 Aristotle

Though he shared in Plato's insight into the unity of the universe, Aristotle, Plato's pupil *par excellence,* thought of it in a rather different way. Aristotle rejected Plato's conviction that Forms somehow exist in their own right, and instead conceived a universe composed of ultimate units that are dynamic sources of activity engaged in causal relationships with each other. These ultimate units of being and originative activity, historically referred to in Latin or English as *substances,*[2] ranged from pure intelligences with attractive power over the heavens, through all manner of living things, to the most passive of earthly elements. For him, unlike for Plato, forms or patterns of existing lie solely within these substances, not in a realm apart.

For Aristotle, to understand any process of nature is chiefly to grasp it in its *causes.* It is causal influence, in one form or another, that binds the whole universe together into an intelligible whole. The ultimate causal influence, he concluded, lies in the attractive power of purely immaterial beings, intelligences, whose proper activity is nothing other than self-reflective contemplation.

The universe, then, is a kind of organism whose various parts act causally upon one another in such a way as to tend toward their own self-fulfillment. This organic conception of the universe is mirrored within the human being, whose bodily functions all work toward a common aim of fulfillment, and who deliberately and consciously aims at the happiness of possessing the truth through contemplative insight.

2. "Substance" is a most unfortunate and misleading translation for Aristotle's Greek word *ousía,* which would be better rendered in English by "entity" or "being." Because of this historical mischance, Aristotle's substance has long but mistakenly been taken to denote something *static* rather than dynamic and changing.

7.1.3   Thomas Aquinas

Thomas achieved an original insight, thought by some to be the most profound yet attained, that in part adapted the views of Aristotle and the Neo-Platonist Plotinus into a new synthesis that took metaphysical thinking to a new level of profundity and clarity. To the Aristotelian view indicated above, Thomas added as it were a new dimension, only vaguely present in Aristotle, that of the *act of existing*. From this perspective, forms or essences find their meaning only in respect to this act of existing: form or essence as a capacity for existing in a certain limited way, and the act of existing as itself naturally issuing into the interactivity of causality.

Thus the ultimate source of all limited acts of existing is a pure, unlimited act of existing (identified with God) from which every finite being shares its own act of existing by *participation* in this limitless source of all existing. Such a participation in existing has similarities not only to Plato's participation of the Forms but especially to Plotinus's concept of the *emanation* of being from the One, together with a consequent tendency to return to the One.

This view provides a new and more powerful conceptuality of the unity of the universe, this time in terms of its very act of existing, as well as of the goal of human living which is to return to its very source.[3] Thomas thus takes Aristotle and Plotinus to a new level.

7.1.4   Alfred North Whitehead

Whitehead strove to make intelligible sense of the ongoing rush of temporal events, and to do it in terms of the creative becoming or "process" that he recognized introspectively within his own immediate experience. Human experience is heavy with a sense of the flow of time, of value or importance, of the influence of the immediate past on the present, and of a certain degree of freedom in

---

3. See the fine volume by Oliva Blanchette, *The Perfection of the Universe According to Aquinas.*

responding creatively to that past in forming a novel future. The whole ongoing universe is conceived to consist of individual centers of experience causally interwoven in their thrust toward the future, and human experience is taken as a kind of sophisticated model of all such acts, no matter how primitive those acts might be. In accounting for both the stability and the emerging novelty evident in the temporal world, Whitehead also found it necessary to suppose the continual influence of a unique, everlasting center of experience (which he called "God") that fallibly lures the process of the world by attraction, not by coercion. Thus the flow of our own immediate experience, coupled with the metaphysical necessity both of a timeless background of stability and of a source for the emergence of novelty, provides the key to understanding the whole process of the universe.

7.2   OBJECTIONS AGAINST THE VERY POSSIBILITY OF METAPHYSICS

In the preceding section, in perhaps shameful over-simplicity, I have attempted to identify the basic metaphysical insights of four great metaphysicians of widely different eras. They all share the presupposition that reality is intelligible and value laden, and that it is worth while to engage in such speculation. Do these metaphysical viewpoints amount to a kind of knowing? In fact do they amount to anything at all worth doing? There is a strong tradition in the history of philosophy that says they don't. According to it, metaphysics ranges from the impossible to the meaningless. If that is right, then it is an exercise in futility to examine the particular views of the above thinkers as possible instances of ways of knowing. Let us therefore examine more closely the soundness of the main objections that have been raised against the very possibility of metaphysics. If the objections are less than convincing, we may reasonably examine the alternative view by considering the positive reasons for thinking that metaphysical thinking can indeed constitute a kind of knowing.

7.2.1 David Hume's objection

Among the historical objections we may well begin with that of David Hume. Hume thinks that it is for reasons of vanity and superstition that people pry into matters that are really inaccessible to the powers of human reason, and that they do not give up the enterprise just because they have not yet succeeded. (As in gambling, I suppose, there is always the hope that the next effort will finally pay off.) So Hume thinks it useful to save us the trouble of attempting to formulate a metaphysics by proving ahead of time that such an enterprise cannot possibly succeed.[4]

The reason it cannot, Hume thinks, is simple. The metaphysician supposes that he or she is reaching conclusions about profound matters of fact, about the deep structure of all reality, whereas the mathematician more modestly restricts his assertions to the abstract realm of ideas and consequently can produce real demonstrations. The mathematician can show not only that a mathematical relation is true but that it is necessarily true. That is what a demonstration does. Pythagoras demonstrated that the square on the hypotenuse does not just happen to equal the sum of the squares on the two sides but that it could not possibly be otherwise. But Pythagoras, as we have noted earlier, was not talking about physically factual "triangles," for there are none, but about abstract, ideal triangles, things of the mind. Now, argues Hume, there can be no real demonstrations about factual, as distinguished from purely ideal, reality as the metaphysician supposes, for the very good reason that matters of fact always *could* be otherwise.

Furthermore, Hume believes that ideas are only faint images either of the sense impressions that gave rise to them or of the very workings of the mind. At the same time he restricts the content of

4. There is a mathematical instance of something like Hume's strategy here. Most of us, having learned in high school how to bisect an angle with nothing more than dividers and a straight edge, have tried our hand at *tri*secting an angle using only the same tools. We did not succeed, but perhaps kept on trying. But I understand that it has been demonstrated by topologists that such an enterprise is impossible. Thus, knowing the futility of it we are saved the time and trouble of trying to do what can't be done.

sense impressions to clean-cut *sensa* such as colors and sounds. Consequently he is forced to conclude that our feeling of *causal influence* of the world upon us, or of the causal continuity of our personal identity over time, can be only a reflection of habits of the mind, since there is no sense impression of causal *influence* that is on a par with impressions of color and sound. There can therefore be no metaphysics that legitimately acknowledges causal connectedness within nature or, consequently, a continuity of personal identity over time. Hume's devastating conclusion was that any book on metaphysics is fit only for the flames since it deals neither with the pure relations of abstract ideas nor with any necessary relations actually found in experienced nature.[5]

7.2.2   Immanuel Kant's objection

Kant raised Hume's conclusion to another plane. He proposed, with intimidating complexity, that the metaphysician's ideal of discovering the intrinsic—and hence universal—structure of reality is an illusion, not because, as Hume says, we cannot penetrate so far, but because even if we could we would find that we are only looking at the reflection of our own minds. The only world we can encounter is a world that is largely of our own making, not a world in itself, because the experienced world has already been structured by our own powers of knowing. When we identify causal relationships between events in nature, we really are discovering nature as our minds have molded it.[6] Consequently, claims Kant, the only

---

5. The above ideas can be found in Hume's *Enquiry Concerning Human Understanding*.

6. If at this point you are wondering what the difference is between the outlooks of Hume and Kant, you might think of it this way. Hume supposes that he is confronted with an appearing world—or more accurately, with a set of succeeding appearances—onto which his mind then proceeds, by natural habit, to lay an interpretation of causal connection. Thus although a pure succession of appearances is all he really finds himself confronted with, his acquired habit of mind produces the illusion that the events themselves are causally connected. Yet the connection is really only in the mind. For Kant, however, the given, appearing world, or the set of appearances, *is itself causally structured,* though Kant thinks that in fact that causal structure

legitimate metaphysics is a study of the necessary structures for the very possibility of experience at all, and these are structures of the mind. Metaphysics, then, must be turned inward and become a study of the mind if it is to have any future legitimacy.[7]

7.2.3 Logical positivism's objection

Though there are variants to the logical positivist position, a lucid example of the general thrust of its "abolition" of metaphysics is laid out by Alfred Jules Ayer (1910–1989) in his early and rather sensational book, *Language, Truth and Logic.* His focus is on *meaning*: on the meaning of "meaning" and on its relation to the truth of assertions. The seminal idea is that meaningfulness is already pre-supposed by the notions of truth or falsity. Hence the first question about a purported statement is not whether or not it is true but whether it has meaning, whether it really says anything at all or only appears to do so. We would waste our time, for instance, if we considered whether the utterance, "A ton is bigger than a mile," is true or false since it has no sense—is literally nonsense—in the first place. We must therefore adopt some standard of meaningfulness and then test assertions against it before we can proceed to judge their truth or falsity.

Ayer borrows his principle of meaningfulness from the early thought of Ludwig Wittgenstein (1889–1951) and from the group of thinkers who came to be known as "The Vienna Circle." Their criterion of meaningfulness was called a "verification principle," which might more clearly be called a principle of testability. Very roughly it states that if a proposition does not confine itself to abstract relationships (such as those of mathematics or logic) but

---

must have been antecedently imparted by the mind to the experienced world as a necessary condition of the very possibility of intelligible experience. There is no experienced world that is not already causally structured, yet that structure reflects not a world in itself but what the mind already brought to the experience.

7. Kant works out this position in massive detail in his celebrated *Critique of Pure Reason,* and suggests it more briefly in his *Prolegomena to Any Future Metaphysics.*

claims to assert an existential fact, and if furthermore there is no conceivable way that one might test through the senses whether that proposition is true or not, then there is literally no sense or meaning in that utterance in the first place. It is only noise or words masquerading as an assertion.

Ayer's early version of the verification principle runs as follows:

> I require of an empirical hypothesis, not indeed that it should be conclusively verifiable, but that some possible sense-experience should be relevant to the determination of its truth or falsehood. If a putative proposition fails to satisfy this principle, and is not a tautology, then I hold that it is metaphysical, and that, being metaphysical, it is neither true nor false but literally senseless.[8]

The proposition, for instance, that the planet Pluto is made of green cheese, while absurdly false, is meaningful because we know in general how we would go about physically checking on its truth even though we might not presently be able or even interested to do it. Only because the proposition is meaningful do we also think it ridiculously false. Every single one of the traditional propositions of metaphysics, however, is thought by Ayer to fail this criterion of testability. For they all purport to assert something about the factual world, yet there is no conceivable empirical test that would either confirm or falsify them. How shall we run an observational test, in the laboratory or out, that would experimentally determine whether God exists, or the will is free, or the human soul is immortal? According to Ayer, the project of metaphysics is not, as Hume had thought, unattainable because it exceeds the power of the mind but rather because it literally makes no sense in the first place.

---

8. Alfred Jules Ayer, *Language, Truth and Logic,* 31. In the second edition of this book after reflecting on ten years of criticism, Ayer makes an involved and subtle revision of the exact form of the verification principle he wishes to adopt. It suffices for our present purposes, however, to deal with the simpler, original formulation, and doing so will not vitiate our eventual criticism of it, because our argument will tell equally well against either formulation.

There can be no meaningful answers to the above questions because the questions themselves are nonsense.

What then shall we make of Plato's affirmation of the existence of the Forms, or Aristotle's of substantial form, or Aquinas's of participation in the act of existing, or Whitehead's analysis of his postulated "actual entities"? On Ayer's view such assertions are all nonsense, the product of failing to grasp the natural limits of meaning. The same would apply to Kant's labyrinthine structures of pure reason. Tell me, Herr Professor Dr. Kant, how do you empirically test whether or not the experienced world is already structured by the formalities of the mind? Since that is clearly impossible, you have been speaking nonsense in proposing this. We just have the world that presents itself to us empirically, and we delude ourselves if we suppose there is any sense or meaning in trying to get behind that.

7.2.4 Ludwig Wittgenstein's objections

In his earlier major work, *Tractatus Logico-Philosophicus* (1922), Wittgenstein had explored the capacity of language to picture fact. In his later *Philosophical Investigations* (published posthumously in 1953) he abandoned that approach and pursued the implications of regarding language as comparable to a *game* we play according to accepted rules. In neither view did he find any literal sense in the sort of questions and conclusions traditionally embodied in metaphysics. Here is a clear expression of Wittgenstein's later view on this matter:

> For Wittgenstein it is language-games which embody both the categorical features of the world which philosophers have called metaphysical features, and also the features of knowing which philosophers have called epistemological. In short, . . . it is the *possibilities of meaning* which establish both the ontological and the epistemological, and not, as in traditional philosophy, the other way around.
>
> What have been regarded as "different kinds of being," in Wittgenstein's philosophy appear as "different ways of speaking"

or different language-games. Thus, for example, the differences between a thing, a quality, a relation, . . . a sensation, an emotion, a motive, an impulse, a disposition, . . . appear as different grammatical possibilities or different language-games. . . . We are not . . . confronted by "different kinds of realities," but rather by "different possibilities of speaking."[9]

The assertion, then, is that the natural evolution of language has enabled us to use such words as those cited above to communicate with each other in accepted ways. We get along in the common sense world by employing such words, but we deceive ourselves if we suppose that each of them names some object that we can somehow know about independently of what we say about it.

When with Wittgenstein we thus turn our attention to the kind of language-games we play when we talk of Platonic Forms, or of the act of existing, or of the intrinsic constitution of a Whiteheadian actual entity, what can we conclude but that some of us happen to enjoy playing a kind of mental chess with such concepts? What can possibly be its relevance to human affairs? If there is no sense in this, then the whole inquiry of this book is not even a case of barking up the wrong tree, since we are in no position to know any trees independent of the barking, but rather a barking that misconceives what barking is all about.[10]

For many contemporary philosophers Wittgenstein's insights have seemed to usher in a new dawn for a philosophic enterprise long darkened by confusion. Indeed, for some the experience has been little short of euphoric, as we gather from the following effusion:

In the past fifteen or twenty years, important things have happened in philosophy. Where darkness ruled before, it now seems that one can not only hope for light but also sense its

---

9. Henry Le Roy Finch, *Wittgenstein—The Later Philosophy,* 79; emphasis in original.

10. I understand that a recent study concluded that dogs bark mainly because they enjoy it. Perhaps the same should be said of metaphysicians.

approach, and even, here and there, catch a glimpse of it. . . .The decisive point—that at which we came to see things in a new light and in a new way—has nearly always been a demonstration of the way the expressions concerned have been misunderstood, or, in Wittgenstein's terms, have been supposed to belong to the wrong language-game. All this is due to Wittgenstein's teaching.[11]

7.2.5 The problem of arbitrariness

Finally, let me spell out an objection to the possibility of metaphysics that can be drawn from the argument developed in the previous chapters, an objection that may already have occurred to the reader. It would go something like this. The respective philosophies of Plato, Aristotle, Thomas Aquinas, and Whitehead have been put forward as first-rate examples of the enterprise of metaphysics. But it is obvious that those philosophies are mutually incompatible. They disagree with one another as to fundamentals. Each philosophic viewpoint is self-contained within the horizon defined by its own distinctive conceptual structure (what I have termed its discovery structure). Those philosophic perspectives on reality are radically distinct and in a real sense *incommensurable* with one another. But then at most one of them—and perhaps none—can adequately reflect reality. And even if one is in fact the true one, how shall we know which it is? Would not a workable criterion for arriving at such a discernment have, itself, the status of a discovery structure on a higher level, a kind of meta-discovery-structure? And what shall be the criterion for accepting that meta-structure? Are we not involved here in an infinite regress or else in circular reasoning, so that in fact we simply accept one system rather than another for no justifiable reason at all? And how would a viewpoint adopted in that fashion deserve the name of knowing? It would seem that all metaphysical

11. Justus Hartnack, *Wittgenstein and Modern Philosophy,* 103.

systems must suffer from an ultimate arbitrariness that vitiates their claim to be ways of knowing.

7.2.6   Can the enterprise of this present essay survive such criticisms?

I think it can and I propose to give arguments why. In any event, the above challenges have driven our considerations to the bed rock of philosophy, the point at which each thinker must take a stand. Archimedes, on becoming aware of the principle of the lever, is said to have exclaimed that if you gave him a place to stand he could move the world. The above challenges, especially Wittgenstein's, amount to asserting that a starting point for metaphysics in the traditional sense is as unattainable as Archimedes' place to put his world lever. And if it is not, it is at any rate a matter of arbitrary choice, not of demonstration. For the starting point is the ground of all demonstrations and the conclusion of none.

In the chapter that follows I shall respond to these objections and give reasons for thinking that what we have been about here, and in general what metaphysics is all about, is plausibly an investigation of reality that has sense.

QUESTIONS FOR REVIEW AND DISCUSSION

1. How do you express to yourself Bergson's distinction between the "soul" of a philosophy and its conceptual expression? Do you think it is plausible?

2. How does Plato's view of the unity of experienced nature relate to his view of values?

3. What is the new "dimension" of analysis by which Thomas Aquinas goes beyond Aristotle?

4. Why is there need to account both for the stability of the universe and its novelty?

5. Whitehead thought it necessary to ground the source of both stability and novelty in the *same* being. Can you think why this seems reasonable or necessary?

6. In what sense does Hume think metaphysics must be impossible, and why?

7. In what way does Kant's criticism of metaphysics go deeper than that of Hume?

8. How do the logical positivists reorient the question and its solution?

9. How does Wittgenstein's position fit in here?

10. Why does metaphysics, regarded as an ultimate perspective on reality, appear logically impossible from the outset? How does one evade this perplexity?

chapter 8

PHILOSOPHIC KNOWING, PART II: METAPHYSICS ALIVE

In the first chapter I described philosophy as "an activity of the human mind by which we inquire into the ultimate intelligible structure of the world of our experience, including that experience itself. It is an investigation into the ultimate nature and meaning of the experienced world and of our experience of it, an attempt to understand experience in its dimension of value and meaning." I said that this is what Aristotle called "first" or the most fundamental philosophy. It is metaphysics in the proper sense.

If you require a description by a more reputable philosopher, here is how Etienne Gilson put it: "*Metaphysics is the knowledge gathered by a naturally transcendent reason in its search for the first principles, or first causes, of what is given in sensible experience.*"[1] What I shall attempt to show in this final chapter is how metaphysics, in that sense, works itself out in practice, how it survives the objections posed in the previous chapter, and how it was exemplified both in the classic cases we have considered and in this essay itself. Then I shall point to some major metaphysical problems we shall have to leave as an invitation to future explorations.

---

1. Etienne Gilson, *The Unity of Philosophical Experience,* 248; italics in the original.

8.1 THE NATURE OF METAPHYSICS

Both of the descriptions quoted above emphasize analyzing experience, experience as we live it.[2] This after all is where we find ourselves and there is no other starting point for philosophy. But then our reason reaches beyond the sensibility of our experiencing to discover something of its structural principles and causes. This is the sense in which metaphysics claims to be a form of knowing; it is a function of what Gilson meant by the transcendence of reason.

Also, metaphysics aims at understanding primarily for understanding's sake. In doing so it tries to grasp the complexity of experience and the experienced world in the light of a *universal scheme of relationships* such that every instance of experience makes sense in terms of that scheme. It differs from other theoretic inquiries in that it aims to view the experienced world not from this or that selected perspective but from a perspective that leaves nothing out. As Aristotle pointed out, "being" is said in many different ways, but metaphysics aims to understand experience in terms of *being as such,* being in all its ways. Thus it has the widest possible discovery structure and the widest possible horizon, that of all being. At first this might seem to violate the whole notion of understanding in virtue of horizons, since it sounds like an effort to achieve a knowledge not defined by any horizon at all, a horizonless knowledge. In reality, however, the perspective of *being as such* constitutes of itself a unique horizon for metaphysics, distinct from all others.

In order to form that unique discovery structure, it is necessary to devise both intuitive and conceptual frameworks in terms of which we attempt to view being as such. The frameworks are a function of the fundamental *principles* in virtue of which we endeavor to understand experience, leaving out no way of being. Any such first principles are chosen because they seem to correspond

---

2. Here and throughout I am using "experience" in a broad and objectivist, not a Kantian, sense. I assume that an extramental world in fact imposes itself upon us in experience, so that in experience we encounter a world. Hence to inquire into experience is also to inquire into the world, not just into subjectivity.

to experience itself. As first principles they cannot of course be demonstrated (on pain of infinite regress) but they may be taken as even better than demonstrable insofar as they give themselves as evident.

For instance, we may recognize that the world we immediately encounter gives itself as heavy with value or importance, good or bad, and as affecting us by its active influence. We may even extrapolate from our own direct human experience and from the apparent behavior of all living things and suppose that all fundamental beings incline toward their own fulfillment—in other words, that they are in some sense goal-aimed, though not necessarily consciously so. We may also presuppose that it belongs to every being to be dynamic, to be in a state of self-development rather than remain static.

Such presuppositions, many or all of which were accepted by the four philosophers we considered above, determine the metaphysical outlook in a most fundamental way. But there is still required a *conceptual* structure in terms of which to work out in a detailed and communicable way the resulting understanding of reality. As Bergson remarked, concepts are like intellectual snapshots. They depict reality in terms of timeless patterns, so that we can grasp it more readily with our intellects, even though, by their very nature, concepts are blind to the dynamic process of the real.

So every metaphysical system that we have noticed, besides its implicit, intuitive outlook, embodies a connection of interrelated concepts that attempt to capture certain features of the real. Each of the four metaphysical systems described earlier attempts to do this, yet each does it in terms of its own particular conceptual scheme. The Forms of Plato are such instances, as are Aristotle's concept of substance, Thomas's concept of participation in existing, or Whitehead's concept of feelings of fact or of possibility.

These schemes are mutually incommensurable inasmuch as the concepts of one do not correspond, item for item, with those of another. Each embodies a particular scheme of categoreal wholeness, some universal framework of principles. Yet the aim of each system is the same: to give a conceptual account of the structure of any and every reality just insofar as it is a reality. The history of philosophy (in the sense of metaphysics) is the story of repeated efforts to achieve the best universal framework for understanding all of reality.

By what criteria can we judge one metaphysical scheme superior to another? It seems that there is a kind of unavoidable circularity here because any such judging must itself be already a function of a particular perspective or horizon determinative of what is more and what is less believable. This is another form of the fundamental puzzle about the adoption or justification of philosophic first principles. All philosophic reasoning and conclusions rely on first principles which, as such, cannot be demonstrated (otherwise they are not first) but are nevertheless accepted as more nearly correct than their opposites.

The metaphysician is trying to grasp the root intelligibility of experience taken in its wholeness, and so agreement with lived experience must be the ultimate touchstone, both the first and the last, of any metaphysics. Does the metaphysical system allow for the dimension of value, for instance, and for the striving for an aim that characterizes human conscious experience? Does it make room for the emergence of real novelty in the world? In trying to accommodate within a coherent system both these and other aspects of experienced reality, we can only feel our way tentatively toward what seems to be the right direction. We cannot prove our principles, we choose them. As the saying goes, you pays your money and you takes your choice. The only alternative is to give up the undertaking altogether.

If there is an intelligibility inherent within the experienced world, then that intelligibility is worth reaching for, even if we must approach it uncertainly and asymptotically. Radical disagreement among philosophers as to the fundamental character of reality simply entails that they cannot all be right, not that the enterprise is not worth attempting. As Gilson wrote: "If metaphysical speculation is a shooting at the moon, philosophers have always begun by shooting at it; only after missing it have they said that there was no moon, and that it was a waste of time to shoot at it."[3]

8.2 REPLY TO THE OBJECTIONS

In view of the above considerations about the general possibility of a metaphysics, the particular objections that have been brought against it, as described earlier, appear less than convincing.

8.2.1 Reply to Hume

Hume misconceives (1) the nature of metaphysics, (2) the origin of ideas, and (3) the character of immediate experience. He demands that metaphysics be strictly demonstrative if it is to be legitimate at all. He supposes that the content of an idea cannot transcend the sensibility of the impression giving rise to it. And he overlooks that particular dimension of sense experience by which—unlike in our entertaining a display of colors and sounds—we directly *feel* the influence of the immediate past upon us. This experienced sense of causal influence grounds our conviction of an order of the universe and of our own personal identity over time, both of which are indispensable parts of a satisfactory metaphysics.[4]

8.2.2 Reply to Kant

Kant appears to have accepted from the empiricists the representational view of sense perception that we have criticized. He also

---

3. Gilson, *Unity,* 249.

4. In section 3.1 of this book, under the name "fundamental perception," I briefly described this dimension of sense experience wherein we literally feel causal influence. It was spelled out in some detail by Whitehead, who called it "perception in the mode of causal efficacy," chiefly in *Process and Reality* (168–83) and in *Symbolism* (39–52). I believe that Whitehead's articulation of this aspect of sense experience constitutes a major contribution to epistemology, but this is not the place to explain and defend Whitehead's view.

was alarmed by Hume's argument that nature itself cannot be—or at least cannot be known to be—causally connected, one event affecting another. Yet causal connectedness is the necessary ground of the order of nature that science strives to discover. Without it, physical science can have no foundation in fact. It was Kant's misfortune to accept so much from Hume, and his genius to propose a revolutionary solution to the malformed problem he thus found himself faced with.

Kant wanted an experienced world that the new, Newtonian physics could give a demonstrative account of, a world that is causally connected and hence embodies an order of nature describable by deterministic laws of motion. Yet Hume had persuaded him that causal connectedness could not possibly lie *within* the world itself. But the world we experience, the phenomenal world, seemed to Kant to be causally ordered as we experience it, not only as we subsequently interpret it. Kant therefore built his new view on the supposition that the mind itself must have already provided the causal connectedness of the experienced world, and must have provided it a priori, as a necessary condition of the very possibility of intelligible sense experience. In Kant's view, then, all the necessary structure of experience, hence all its ground of intelligibility, has been provided by the mind itself. Consequently the only legitimate study of intelligible structures within experience, hence the only legitimate "metaphysics," must be a study of the structures of the mind itself as necessary conditions for the very possibility of intelligible experience.

In that way Kant endeavored to restore causal continuity, and hence an order of nature, to the phenomenal world studied by physics. According to his conjecture—and it was a conjecture—the causal connectedness actually observed in nature is provided a priori by the mind itself, so that to study nature in its causal continuity amounts to studying the structure of the mind.

Here we are reduced to fundamental options, to philosophic cops and robbers: "Bang, I got you!" "No, you missed me!" If we suppose, with Kant, that the structure of the experienced world can only be due to the constructive activity of the mind, then it is the mind that we must investigate, not nature. But there is no need to make that assumption if we recognize the feeling of causal connectedness as immediately given within sense experience, and if we also have a metaphysical system that can give a plausible account of how one event can itself influence another. (Recall sections 3.1 and 3.2.)

8.2.3   Reply to logical positivism

The objection of the logical positivists against metaphysics fares much worse than Kant's. Everything depends upon the acceptability of the verification principle. But why should we accept that principle as the ultimate criterion of meaning? The principle arbitrarily decrees that statements can carry no meaning unless they are either tautologies or are sensibly testable. But the verification principle itself is surely not sensibly testable. Is it then a tautology? Is it indeed self-evident that this is exactly and only what meaningfulness can amount to? Acceptance of the principle is purely gratuitous, an option that one need not make but only chooses to make. The metaphysician may be excused for refusing to subscribe to such a narrow conception of meaning with its correspondingly narrow conception of the world.

8.2.4   Reply to Wittgenstein

But what shall we say about the position of the later Wittgenstein? Have we really to do only with the structure of language rather than with a world? Is it true, as we saw Finch write earlier, that "it is the *possibilities of meaning* which establish both the ontological and the epistemological, and not, as in traditional philosophy, the other way around"?

But what can ground these possibilities of meaning if not the very structure of reality itself? I simply do not find it evident or even believable that language really does come first, and that thought cannot be independent of and precede the structural constrictions of language. When we struggle to give linguistic expression to our deepest thoughts, is this not a sign not only that words and concepts are sometimes inadequate for expressing thought, but that the thought we struggle to express antecedes language? Why must we suppose that our difficulty in giving words to our insights into the depths of the universe or of our experience arises solely from misusing the ordinary rules of language? There is not the least reason for presupposing that ordinary language and its vocabulary, even when rightly used, is already adequate to express the most fundamental aspects of reality.

8.2.5 Reply to the problem of arbitrariness

What, finally, can be replied to the last objection (7.2.5), imputing an inevitable arbitrariness or circularity to any metaphysical view in such a fundamental way as to vitiate its claim to be a form of knowledge? Well, the basic reply to this objection was already furnished in section 8.1. There can be no demonstrating of philosophic first principles, there is only an intuitively informed choice. But the same is true of scientific first principles. All human knowledge of any sort is inadequate to the fullness of the being it attempts to understand, and conceptual knowledge is at best a faint approximation of the real. Yet intuitive and conceptual schemes do reveal something of reality. We do not *know* this of any metaphysical system but we recognize it inasmuch as it to some degree renders intelligible to us the richness of our immediate experience.

8.3 CLASSICAL METAPHYSICS AS INSTANCES OF KNOWING

In light of all the above, let us take another brief look at the classical, historical instances of metaphysics that we pointed to earlier, and see whether, and in what respect, they seem to amount to a kind of knowledge.

We noted in the previous chapter that Plato told us that he had never set down on paper his deepest thoughts. But I think it fair to say that he was deeply preoccupied with the tension in experienced reality between change and the changeless. As is well known, he thought the heart of reality lies in immutable Forms that somehow derive from an immutable Good or One, and that change is due to the imperfect participation in these Forms on the part of material things.

I do not know of any contemporary philosophers who hold literally to Plato's theory of Forms, yet most of them are, as it seems to me, fundamentally Platonist in their philosophic outlooks. If this is indeed the case, then Plato's metaphysics, which lurks under everything he wrote, identifies and at least partially succeeds in rendering intelligible some of the most fundamental aspects of reality and of the human mind. How could it be plausibly supposed that Plato's conception of reality has nothing of truth to it, that it does not amount to at least some kind of knowledge, some intellectual or perhaps intuitional grasp of the structure of reality? The enduring attraction of Plato's thought would be inexplicable if one were to deny that his metaphysics utterly fails as an attempt at ultimate knowledge.[5]

As for Aristotle's metaphysics, it is enough to notice just two aspects of it that can lay claim to be a form of knowledge. One is his analysis of the general structure of a primary being, the other is his recognition of *potentiality* as an authentic form of being. As was noted in the previous chapter Aristotle, contrary to present misconceptions about what he meant by "substance," conceived the basic units of existence (his "substances" or primary beings) to be dynamic, self-developing, and goal oriented, moving themselves to their own fulfillment.

This general conception enabled Aristotle to give a plausible, detailed account of the human person in its physical and psychological complexity. It also yielded a general conception of nature as an intelligible whole of inter-related instances of becoming and acting. It seems at least plausible that such an account is authentic as far as it goes. If so, then it has illuminated reality for us and so is a form of knowledge.

---

5. This contention, if correct, would have weight against the anti-metaphysical views of thinkers like Hume or the logical positivists; less so perhaps against Wittgenstein; none at all (except in a special sense) against Kant.

The metaphysics of Thomas Aquinas adds a new dimension of intelligibility to that of Aristotle. At a profound new level Thomas, by his theory of participation in the act of existing, discovers a radical unity of the cosmos in its being and its becoming. Such an intuitive grasp of the wholeness of reality constitutes a high point of what it means to know.

Whitehead, finally, brought the traditional conception of metaphysics into a twentieth-century form. Though he calls his principal book (*Process and Reality*) "An Essay in Cosmology," and so presumably only a fragment of a metaphysics, its underlying conceptuality, as tentatively expressed in his "Categoreal Scheme," has most of the breadth, depth, and coherent complexity of metaphysics in the classic sense. The vitality of the contemporary movement in process philosophy, as inspired by Whitehead, is itself evidence that what Whitehead's metaphysics has suggested about the ongoing, processive wholeness of the universe, with its inherent dimension of value, goal-directedness, and freedom, rings true to many who have understood the conceptuality. They find it credible and have good epistemological grounds to do so. They believe, in other words, that Whitehead's metaphysics in fact illuminates what they actually find in experience, and thus is in fact a way of knowing.

8.4 THIS ESSAY AS AN ADVENTURE IN METAPHYSICAL KNOWING

We began our exploration of human knowing with a philosophical analysis of sense perception. We noticed that it cannot be the case that we perceive the extramental world just as it is in itself, but neither is it believable that we perceive not extramental objects but only our own perceptions of them—what I called "the myth of the theater." We developed, rather, a view of what is going on in perception that I call "relational realism." We justified this view in a twofold way: by calling attention to our immediate experience of being affected by other things and by invoking the philosophic principles that the effective causality of a cause is found *within* its effect, and that a causal agent must in some way exist in its own right, be autonomous in its existing, if it is actively to cause. In this way we made sense of how it is that we do indeed immediately perceive an extramental world, but only and exactly in its relation to us in our act of perceiving. We were able to accept our experience of an extramental world as basically authentic. At the same time we justified our belief in the autonomous existence and activity of the objects in that world.

So we applied metaphysical principles to our immediate experience and in that way illuminated that experience to our inquiring minds. This was not only applying metaphysics, it was a genuine form of knowing since it revealed to us something of the intelligibility of both the world and our own experiencing.

So also in the course of our considerations it became increasingly clear that the world we experience, and our experiencing itself, transcend the purely physical. Our knowing, and even our perceiving, can't be wholly explained only in terms of brain functioning, even though that may be a necessary condition for perceiving and knowing. As there is more to our perceiving and knowing than brain activity, so there is more to the beings that we experience and understand than what we find in their physicality, their here and now particularity. In the objects that we perceive we recognize patterns that are not exhausted in their individual selves, and we find our own inquiring minds not boxed in by particulars. Rather, we find our minds aimed at existence in any form, and we find the things of our experience reaching beyond themselves in their acting.

This is surely a beginning of metaphysical knowing, yet it leaves all sorts of philosophic problems yet to be dealt with. They constitute an implicit invitation to future metaphysical thought. For instance, how shall we account for the twofold aspect of our own personal activity, physical and mental, while at the same time respecting our unity as a person? I reject, as I hope the reader does, Descartes's splitting of the human person into separate *substances,* mental and physical. In what other sense, then, can we be both physical and mental beings?

Again, how shall we account for our experience of being part of the universe and the universe part of us? What makes up the unity of the universe of which we feel ourselves a part? And to what can we attribute the value dimension that we experience in the world?

What we have uncovered about the discovery structure and the horizon of metaphysics makes plausible that problems like these are real problems worth trying to solve. To the extent that we succeed we shall better understand both the world and ourselves, and that is knowing indeed. Yet the solution to such problems is for us never quite formalizable. As Bergson wrote, "A philosopher worthy of the name has never said more than a single thing: and even then it is something he has tried to say, rather than actually said."[6]

Whitehead was of a similar mind. Here is what he wrote:

> Philosophy begins in wonder. And, at the end, when philosophic thought has done its best, the wonder remains. There have been added, however, some grasp of the immensity of things. . . . The aim at philosophic understanding is the aim at piercing the blindness of activity in respect to its transcendent functions.[7]

And in another place:

> Philosophy is mystical. For mysticism is direct insight into depths as yet unspoken. But the purpose of philosophy is to rationalize mysticism: not by explaining it away, but by the introduction of novel verbal characterizations, rationally coör-dinated.
>
> Philosophy is akin to poetry, and both of them seek to express that ultimate good sense which we term civilization. In each case there is reference to form beyond the direct meanings of words.[8]

6. Henri Bergson, *The Creative Mind,* 112.
7. Alfred North Whitehead, *Modes of Thought,* 168–69.
8. Ibid., 174.

The poet T. S. Eliot, himself a trained philosopher, described it best, I think, when he wrote, toward the end of *Four Quartets*:

> We shall not cease from exploration
> And the end of all our exploring
> Will be to arrive where we started
> And know the place for the first time.[9]

9. T. S. Eliot, *Four Quartets,* "Little Gidding," 59.

BIBLIOGRAPHY

Aristotle. *Metaphysics*. Translated by Richard Hope. Ann Arbor: University of Michigan Press, 1960.

———. *Physics*. Translated by W.D. Ross. In *The Basic Works of Aristotle,* edited by R. McKeon. New York: Random House, 1941.

Ayer, Alfred Jules. *Language, Truth and Logic*. 2nd edition. New York: Dover, 1952.

Bergson, Henri. *The Creative Mind*. Totowa, New Jersey: Littlefield, Adams & Co., 1975.

Blanchette, Oliva. *The Perfection of the Universe According to Aquinas: A Teleological Cosmology*. University Park: Pennsylvania State University, 1992.

Chisholm, Roderick M. *Theory of Knowledge*. 3rd edition. Englewood Cliffs, New Jersey: Prentice-Hall, 1989.

Churchland, Paul M. *Matter and Consciousness: A Contemporary Introduction to the Philosophy of Mind*. Cambridge, Massachusetts: MIT Press, 1984.

Clarke, W. Norris, S.J. "Action as the Self-Revelation of Being: A Central Theme in the Thought of St. Thomas." In *History of Philosophy in the Making,* edited by Linus J. Thro, S.J. Washington, DC: University Press of America, 1982.

———. *Explorations in Metaphysics*. Notre Dame, Indiana: University of Notre Dame Press, 1994.

———. *Person and Being*. Milwaukee: Marquette University Press, 1993.

Dennett, Daniel C. *Consciousness Explained*. Boston: Little Brown, 1991.

Eddington, Arthur. *The Nature of the Physical World*. Ann Arbor: University of Michigan Press, 1958.

Eliot, T. S. *Four Quartets*. San Diego: Harcourt Brace Jovanovich, 1971.

Felt, James W., S.J. "Whitehead's Misconception of 'Substance' in Aristotle." *Process Studies* 14 (1985): 223–36.

Fetz, Reto Luzius. "Aristotelian and Whiteheadian Conceptions of Actuality: I and II." *Process Studies* 19 (1990): 15–27 and 145–55.

Finch, Henry Le Roy. *Wittgenstein—The Later Philosophy*. Atlantic Highland, New Jersey: Humanities Press, 1977.

Galileo. *Discoveries and Opinions of Galileo*. Edited by Stillman Drake. New York: Anchor Books, 1957.

Gilson, Etienne. *The Unity of Philosophical Experience*. San Francisco: Ignatius Press, 1999.

Hartnack, Justus. *Wittgenstein and Modern Philosophy*. Translated by Maurice Cranston. Garden City, New York: Doubleday Anchor, 1965.

Heelan, Patrick A., S.J. "Horizon, Objectivity and Reality in the Physical Sciences." *International Philosophical Quarterly* 7 (September, 1967): 375–412.

Henle, R. J., S.J. *Theory of Knowledge: A Textbook and Substantive Theory of Epistemology*. Chicago: Loyola University Press, 1983.

Hobbes, Thomas. *Human Nature*. In *The English Works of Thomas Hobbes of Malmesbury*, vol. 4, edited by William Molesworth. London: J. Bohn, 1966.

Hocking, William Ernst. "Whitehead as I Knew Him." In *Alfred North Whitehead: Essays on His Philosophy*, ed. by George L. Kline. Englewood Cliffs, New Jersey: Prentice-Hall, 1963.

Hopkins, Gerard Manley. *The Poems of Gerard Manley Hopkins*. Edited by W.H. Garner and N.H. Mackenzie. London: Oxford University Press, 1989.

Hume, David. *An Enquiry Concerning Human Understanding*. Amherst, New York: Prometheus Books, 1988.

———. *A Treatise of Human Nature*. Oxford: Oxford University Press, 1968.

Husserl, Edmund. *Cartesian Meditations: An Introduction to Phenomenology*. Translated by Dorion Cairns. The Hague: Martinus Nijhoff, 1960.

Kant, Immanuel. *Critique of Pure Reason*. Translated by Norman Kemp Smith. New York: St. Martin's Press, 1965.

———. *Prolegomena to Any Future Metaphysics*. Translated by Paul Carus, revised by James W. Ellington. Indianapolis: Hackett, 1977.

Kuhn, Thomas S. *The Structure of Scientific Revolutions*. 3rd ed. Chicago: University of Chicago Press, 1996.

Locke, John. *An Essay Concerning Human Understanding*. 2 vols. Edited by Alexander Campbell. New York: Dover, 1959.

Lonergan, Bernard F., S.J. *Insight: A Study of Human Understanding*. New York: Philosophical Library, 1957.

Merleau-Ponty, Maurice. *Phenomenology of Perception*. Translated by Colin Smith. London: Routledge & Kegan Paul, 1962.

————— "The Primacy of Perception and Its Philosophical Consequences." In *The Primacy of Perception and Other Essays*. Translated by James M. Edie. Evanston, Illinois: Northwestern University Press, 1964.

Newton, Isaac. *Opticks*. New York: Dover, 1952.

Plato. "Letter VII." Translated by L. A. Post. In *The Collected Dialogues of Plato, including the Letters,* edited by Edith Hamilton and Huntington Cairns. New York: Bollingen Foundation, 1961.

—————. *Symposium*. Translated by Robin Waterfield. Oxford: Oxford University Press, 1994.

Pols, Edward. *Radical Realism: Direct Knowing in Science and Philosophy*. Ithaca, New York: Cornell University Press, 1992.

Russell, Bertrand. *Portraits from Memory, and Other Essays*. New York: Simon and Schuster, 1956.

—————. *The Problems of Philosophy*. Oxford: Oxford University Press, 1912.

Searle, John. *Intentionality: An Essay in the Philosophy of Mind*. Cambridge: Cambridge University Press, 1983.

————— *The Mystery of Consciousness*. New York: New York Review of Books, 1997.

Whitehead, Alfred North. *Adventures of Ideas*. New York: Macmillan, 1933.

—————. *Modes of Thought*. New York: Free Press, 1966.

—————. *Process and Reality: An Essay in Cosmology*. Corrected Edition. New York: Free Press, 1978.

—————. *Symbolism: Its Meaning and Effect*. New York: Capricorn Books, 1959.

Wittgenstein, Ludwig. *Philosophical Investigations*. New York: Macmillan, 1958.

—————. *Tractatus Logico-Philosophicus*. London: Routledge & Kegan Paul, 1961.

INDEX

agent (activating) intellect, 64n
aims: and the grasp of possibility, 71; and the problem of unrealized aims, 72
appearance-reality dichotomy, as in Hobbes, Locke, Russell, 21–22
appearances as a medium *in* which or *by* which, 29
appearing (relational) objects distinct from appearances of objects, 24
Aquinas. *See* Thomas Aquinas
Aristotle: on efficient causality as in the effect, 26–27; his epistemology, 25n11; on "first philosophy," 2; his philosophy of an organic, causally connected universe, 94
Ayer, A. J., his critique of metaphysics (that of logical positivism), 99–101

Bergson, Henri, on two aspects of a philosophy (central insight and conceptualization), 92, 109
Berkeley, George, his idealism, 23

brain functioning, as cause or as necessary condition of consciousness, 5–9

causality, efficient: as in its effect (Aristotle), 41–43; experienced (felt), 27; inconsistency of modern interpretation, 42–43; and the myth of the theater, 25–27
Chisholm, Roderick, on appearances and objects of perception, 29n
Churchland, Paul M.: and epistemological reductionism, 4n; and introspection, 15n
Clarke, W. Norris: and the social nature of the person, 70n4; and the term "relational realism," 28n
consciousness and brain functioning, how related? 5–9

Dennett, Daniel, on brain states and consciousness, 7

JAMES W. FELT, S.J., is John Nobili Professor of Philosophy at Santa Clara University.